ESSENTIAL
MUIR

ESSENTIAL MUIR

MUIR

A SELECTION OF JOHN MUIR'S BEST (AND WORST) WRITINGS

Edited with an Introduction by
FRED D. WHITE

Foreword by
JOLIE VARELA

Heyday, Berkeley, California

Originally published in conjunction with Santa Clara University as part of the California Legacy series.

Introduction © 2021, 2006 by Fred D. White
Foreword © 2021 by Jolie Varela

Library of Congress Cataloging-in-Publication Data

Names: Muir, John, 1838- author. | White, Fred D., 1943- editor.
Title: Essential muir : a selection of John Muir's best (and worst) writings / edited with an Introduction by Fred D. White ; foreword by Jolie Varela.
Description: Berkeley : Heyday, [2021]
Identifiers: LCCN 2021017975 (print) | LCCN 2021017976 (ebook) | ISBN 9781597145503 (paperback) | ISBN 9781597145541 (epub)
Subjects: LCSH: Muir, John, 1838-1914. | Natural history--United States. | Naturalists--United States--Biography. | Conservationists--United States--Biography.
Classification: LCC QH31.M9 A3 2021 (print) | LCC QH31.M9 (ebook) | DDC
    508.73--dc23
LC record available at https://lccn.loc.gov/2021017975
LC ebook record available at https://lccn.loc.gov/2021017976

Cover Design: Ashley Ingram
Interior Design: Philip Krayna, PKD, Berkeley
Typesetting: Lorraine Rath

Published by Heyday
P.O. Box 9145, Berkeley, California 94709
(510) 549-3564
heydaybooks.com

Printed in East Peoria, Illinois, by Versa Press, Inc.

10 9 8 7 6 5 4 3 2 1

To Terry Beers and Malcolm Margolin,
for believing I could do this

To my wife, Therese, for her inspiration

And to the spirit of John Muir

Contents

Foreword

Jolie Varela

I started up the Rock Creek trail enjoying the sun and anticipating the seven-mile hike ahead. Just a few feet up I saw a family scrambling for a photo in front of the John Muir Wilderness sign. They watched me approach and I already knew they would ask me to take their photo in front of the sign—a sign that I feel erases my people's history in the so-called Sierra Nevada. To understand the history, we have to go back, and I mean way back. Before John Muir, and before the mountains were renamed the Sierra Nevada by Padre Pedro Font, a Spanish colonizer.

I am Nüümü, better known by our government name as Paiute. My people have lived among the mountains for thousands and thousands of years. Before the mountains were called the Sierra Nevada by colonizers, they were called Pamidu Toiyabe—meaning "the western mountains"—by my ancestors. From the valley we call home, the mountains sit to the west of us. Payahuunadü eventually came to be known as Owens Valley, after Richard Owens, who never actually set foot there. Today, people come from all over the world to recreate on our homelands, but Payahuunadü, "the place of flowing water," is home to our creation. My relatives were born in places like the Buttermilk area and the Owens River Gorge, which are now commonly recognized as climbing destinations. No matter how colonizer names have tried to replace and erase our histories, these lands are our homelands. These new colonial names can't sever ancient connections.

My people, along with those from neighboring tribes, would travel the Pamidu Toiyabe for trade and ceremony. Each tribe would have a name in its own language for the trails and mountains. What is more commonly known as the John Muir Trail today is sprinkled with artifacts from this time. You can find arrowheads and chipped obsidian all along the trail. I've seen grinding stones and abalone as well. In an act of reclamation and responsibility to tell the true story of the trail, we call the trail the Nüümü Poyo, which means "the people's trail." John Muir followed trails that were already there. Even though we, as people Indigenous to these lands, know this truth, it is a truth that many John Muir enthusiasts would vehemently deny. John Muir's legacy as "the Father of Our National Parks" erases the stewardship and connection that Indigenous people, my people, have had on the land for millennia. I would also dare to say that, because of John Muir's views of Native peoples as "dirty," "lazy," and having no place in the pristine wilderness, he is in part responsible for the removal and genocide of the Indigenous people throughout the so-called Sierra Nevada. The stories I've heard about John Muir are a lot different than the stories most people read about in books. Our stories are passed on by word of mouth and not written down anywhere. Many people would argue that this doesn't help with credulity, but English is not my people's first language, and we have always passed down our knowledge and stories through oral tradition. Many people believe that Muir went off into the woods with nothing but "a loaf of bread and a pound of tea." A Native elder shared stories she had heard as a child that tell a very different story. Muir relied heavily on the Indigenous people of the Pamidu Toiyabe. Not only did he follow our trails, he traded for our food, and I'm told that at times he even stole it.

When I was asked to write the foreword for this book I thought, "Oh great, another book about Muir." Aren't there enough John Muir quotes floating around in the world? John Muir quotes are like the *live laugh love* of the conservation world. "The mountains are calling," says nearly every outdoor enthusiast's Instagram bio. When I was told this book would be both the best and worst of Muir, however, I was intrigued. Muir is usually painted as this mystical gray-bearded old man roaming the Sierra Nevada with nothing but a loaf of bread and a walking stick, and people romanticize the hell out of that image. I'm writing this foreword because it allows me to tell the true history of the trail, my people's history, which existed long before Muir.

Muir was racist. It's all right there in his own writing. A common argument is that Muir was a product of his time. But during that time there were also a lot of people who understood that racism was bad.

I started Indigenous Women Hike in 2017 as an act of reclamation—not only reclaiming land and names but also sacred spaces inside of ourselves. Connecting to our lands has been an incredibly healing experience for myself and other women involved. In 2018, we traveled the Nüümü Poyo without permits, because we don't need permission to travel lands we have been and will always be a part of. While we are reminded constantly by wilderness signs that our lands are colonized and our Indigenous names have been changed, we know the truth and we hold the history in our DNA.

I got closer to the sign, and the man I assumed was the grandfather asked me to take his family's photo, just as I had expected. As I was taking their photo I told them I was also going to give them a short history lesson. I told them that John Muir actually followed trails that were already there. These are trade routes that have been used by Indigenous people for thousands of years. These trails were made by my Nüümü ancestors, more commonly known as Paiutes, as well as by other tribes in these mountains who also still exist today. John Muir didn't have a lot of nice things to say about my ancestors. I handed back the phone and the man told me that he had been coming to the Sierra for thirty years and had no idea about these truths, but that they made so much sense. The people thanked me for the history lesson and I set off on the trail to enjoy my hike on my homelands.

Introduction

Determining what is "essential" among a major author's works might just be a classic exercise in futility, or at least a classic impertinence, were it not for the likelihood that such winnowing can serve an important educational function. In the case of John Muir (1838–1914), selecting these essential writings is a means of reassessing the importance of an author whose reputation is not quite where it should be. He has been characterized (and caricatured) as a half-cracked hobo who waxed ecstatic in thunderstorms and earthquakes; who foolishly risked his life to experience a glacier or a waterfall up close; who preferred the society of squirrels and trees to people. He has been labeled a Transcendentalist mystic who over-rhapsodized the sublime beauty of wilderness, confusing the boundary between the natural and the supernatural. He has been considered a crotchety activist who would rather deprive a major city (San Francisco) of water than impede the flow of the Tuolumne River through an uninhabited (so Muir assumed) region (Hetch Hetchy Valley, just north of Yosemite Valley). He is sometimes regarded as an arrogant representative of Manifest Destiny, wishing to preserve land for white settlers even as the forced relocation and genocide of California's Native peoples continued. But Muir's legacy is too complex and important to be diminished by caricature and oversimplification.

Muir once described himself as a "poetico-trampo-geologist-botanist and ornithologist-naturalist." It sounds whimsical, yes, but it nicely reflects his desire to fuse rational and investigative sensibilities with aesthetic and spiritual ideas—to be both naturalist *and* nature celebrant. Why should scientific scrutiny of natural phenomena not be in harmony with worshiping nature's beauty, mystery, and power? Like Thoreau, Muir shrugged off the trappings of materialistic living and pursued his own experiment in living simply and deliberately, according to his internal moral compass.

Everywhere he looked, nature revealed its glory. ("Glorious" was Muir's favorite word; it was used to excess, many would agree, but it best captured his exalted feelings about the wild.) Like the Bible, nature conveyed to him sacred revelations, as when he climbed a giant yellow ponderosa pine in the Yosemite Valley:

> Climbing these grand trees, especially when they are waving and singing in worship in wind-storms, is a glorious experience. Ascending from the lowest branch to the topmost is like stepping up stairs through a blaze of white light, every needle thrilling and shining as if with religious ecstasy.[1]

Muir *ascending*—whether trees, mountains, or glaciers—is Muir in his essence: a man who rejected established religious paths to Heaven, such as the one traveled by his father (who followed the Disciples of Christ[2]), and chose instead to ascend to Heaven via wild nature's path. In choosing this new path to salvation, Muir was not rejecting his Christian faith but extending it, much the way Emerson extended his Christian faith by stepping down as a Unitarian minister and preaching, through poetry and essays, his Transcendentalist credo of finding one's own path to God. As Emerson asserted in his famous (and at the time, notorious) address to the graduating Harvard Divinity School students in 1837:

> Let me admonish you . . . to go alone; to refuse the good models, even those which are sacred in the imagination of men, and dare to love God without mediator or veil. . . . Yourself a new-born bard of the Holy Ghost, cast behind you all conformity, and acquaint men at first hand with Deity.[3]

At a meeting of the American Academy of Arts and Letters in New York in January 1916, Robert Underwood Johnson, an editor and longtime friend of Muir, described Muir's religious beliefs this way:

> The love of nature was his religion, but it was not without a personal God, whom he thought as great in the decoration of a flower as in the launching of a glacier. The old Scotch training persisted through all his studies of causation, and the keynote of his philosophy was intelligent and benevolent design.[4]

Muir's view of nature as infused with spirit, as the very analog of Heaven, is apparent throughout his oeuvre. The tree-climbing passage above is one example; here is another, straight from one of his earliest Yosemite journals. Moved by the power of a waterfall, he records the sublime moment of transport:

> One stupendous unit of light and song, perfect and harmonious as any in heaven. . . . If my soul could get away from this so-called prison, be granted all the list of attributes generally bestowed on spirits, my first ramble on spirit wings . . . I should study Nature's laws.[5]

It is tempting to regard Muir's wilderness quest as a religious quest. However, it may have been, initially, a reaction to his father's unyielding orthodoxy, which included intolerance for intellectual curiosity. Any derelictions of duty brought down the whip. Daniel Muir put his son to the plow at age twelve, forcing him to work sixteen hours a day, six days a week, even when John was ill with the mumps and unable to swallow anything except milk. Only when he contracted pneumonia, as Muir explains in his autobiography, *The Story of My Boyhood and Youth* (1913), was he allowed to remain in bed; but no doctor was called in, "for father . . . believed that God and hard work were by far the best doctors."[6] Muir's assessment of that credo was blunt: "We were all made slaves through the vice of over-industry." It wasn't just "over-industry" but deprivation of liberty as well. Perhaps in his ecstatic responses to finding himself in the wild—he often leaped about, singing, with open arms— Muir was demonstrating, if only to himself, that for the soul to flourish it must break free of all restraint. His siblings, he realized, experienced a similar craving for freedom. When his artist-sister Mary wrote to him in distress after their father had flung her drawings into the mud "to save her soul," Muir promptly sent her enough money to leave home.

What must have been most hurtful to Muir was Daniel's contempt for his son's wilderness explorations. After reading his son's account of a snowstorm atop Mt. Shasta in 1874, Daniel wrote the following to him:

> I knew it was not God's work [you were doing], although you seem to think you are doing God's service. If it had not been for God's boundless mercy you would have been cut off in the midst of your folly.... I know that the world and the church of the world will glory in such as you, but how can they believe which receive honor of one another and seek not the honor that cometh from God only[;] John 5,44. You cannot warm the heart of the saint of God with your cold icy-topped mountains.[7]

Daniel concludes the letter by saying it would be better that John burn his book rather than continue working on it and publishing it, "and then it will do no more harm either to you or to others."

Muir's genius as a nature writer has forged in the public mind the majesty of Sierra and Alaskan wilderness. The mere mention of his name conjures up those majestic emblems of Yosemite— Half Dome, El Capitan, the giant sequoias, the California condor—which in turn conjure up the idea of California itself, as the California state quarter, minted in 2005, attests. However, these associations alone cannot do justice to the polymath and autodidact whose genius also had a technical, mechanical, and rigorously scientific side as well. Long before he began writing, Muir loved inventing—machines that were as practical as they were fanciful. He avidly studied botany and the embryonic sciences of geology and glaciology. And we should not overlook the fact that Muir was from his earliest years also a humanist and a person of compassion—but unfortunately, not always to Indigenous peoples or people of color.

His compassion extended to animals. In fact, some of his most poignant childhood memories involved animals, such as Nob, "the most faithful, intelligent, playful, affectionate, human-like horse I ever knew." He even loved the little black water bugs that congregated on their farm's Fountain Lake—"Their whole lives seemed to be play," he writes in his autobiography, "skimming, swimming, swirling, and waltzing together in little groups."[8] The moral lesson here is that animals are to be respected as kindred spirits: "Thus godlike sympathy grows and thrives and spreads far beyond the teachings of churches and schools, where too often the mean, blinding, loveless doctrine is taught that animals have neither mind nor soul, have no rights that we are bound to respect."[9]

Muir's humanism and compassion for others, however, had some significant shortcomings, largely overlooked by his biographers. In stark contrast to his acute attentiveness to the natural world and to his devotion to the protection of wilderness areas, Muir expressed indifference to, and even at times contempt for, Native peoples. For example, in *The Mountains of California*, Muir alludes to the Indians dwelling at Mono Lake as "mostly ugly, and some of them altogether hideous." We will take a closer look at this flaw in Muir's humanistic views in a moment.

His writings have shaped generations of thought about nature and public lands for both good and ill, and as such his literary art remains a powerful source of insight that deserves continued reflection from our current vantage point.

Muir's Literary Legacy

Not much is known about Muir's sense of his own literary artistry. We do know that he resisted what he referred to disdainfully as "bookmaking." The disdain comes largely from his favoring first-hand experience in the world over vicarious experience derived from books. As he wrote in his journal around 1872, "No amount of word-making will ever make a single soul to know these mountains. . . . One day's exposure to mountains is better than cartloads of books."[10]

The only writing he truly enjoyed was journal writing—field notes and drawings. Writing for publication, however, required confining himself indoors (he dubbed the study in his Martinez home his "scribble den"); it required transmuting his fragmentary, spontaneously generated journal entries into fully developed, coherent discourse. For Muir this was devilishly hard work. Explains Marion Randall Parsons, who boarded Muir when he was working on *Travels in Alaska*, "Composition was always slow and laborious for him. . . . Each sentence, each phrase, each word, underwent his critical scrutiny, not once but twenty times before he was satisfied to let it stand."[11]

But his resistance to writing books is not as paradoxical as it seems. Muir wrote as naturally as he walked and rejoiced in nature—but it was spontaneous writing. His journal was part of his amazingly sparse backpack, accompanied by three books (the New Testament, *Paradise Lost*, and Robert Burns's poems), a change of clothes, and some food. He used pencils to write his journal entries and make sketches; sometimes when he wrote letters, he made his own ink out of tree sap. Muir's writing, we might say, was a kind of spontaneously generated singing from the soul. Writing was as essential a life function to him as walking, seeing, breathing.

For someone who did not regard himself as "a writer," Muir possessed a profoundly poetic sensibility. He recognized this sensibility himself early on, and wondered if he could manifest it by literally writing poetry—but no; the few poems of Muir's that survive make it clear that his poetic soul would not manifest itself in traditional verse.

Page randomly through Muir's writings, and the first thing you will probably notice is the way he shifts almost seamlessly from the rhapsodic to the scientific and back again. In virtually one breath, Muir can rejoice in the celestial power of a Yosemite waterfall and describe plant species with botanical precision. He can be expressive as a giddy child in one paragraph and professorial in the next. Was this symptomatic of a capricious sensibility? My guess is that Muir strove in his writing, as he did in his life, to fuse the two sensibilities together. His works are neither "scientific" nor "literary" in the traditional sense of those terms but a fusion of both.

The most dramatic achievement resulting from this fusion of sensibilities occurred when Muir demonstrated beyond a reasonable doubt the glacial origin of the Yosemite Valley. Not only did he collect geological evidence of, for example, glacial striae (scrapings on rock faces that could only have been caused by glacial movement), but he quite transcended conventional scientific procedure altogether by *living like a glacier*. As he explained in an 1871 letter to his lifelong friend and mentor, the educator and botanist Jeanne Carr:

> I can do much of this ice work in the quiet, and the whole subject is purely physical, so that I can get but little from books. All depends upon the goodness of one's eyes. No scientific book in the world can tell me how this Yosemite granite is put together, or how it has been taken down. Patient observation and constant brooding above the rocks, lying upon them for years as the ice did, is the way to arrive at the truths which are graven so lavishly upon them.[12]

Muir's Racist Views

For the past two decades, scholars have been shedding light on John Muir's views toward persons of color and Native peoples.[13] Muir's attitude toward minorities gained renewed attention in the spring of 2020, triggered in part by a resurgence of the Black Lives Matter movement that followed the brutal murders of African Americans at the hands of police. The reputation of John Muir as America's premier nature celebrant and preservationist must continue to be reassessed in terms of racism, especially toward Indigenous peoples and African Americans. To attempt to absolve him by noting that "this was how people thought back then" is not acceptable; the legions of white abolitionists and defenders of the rights of Native Americans to their own lands also lived "back then." To some extent, Muir's racial biases evolved in his later years, but he never repudiated his earlier racist attitudes.

According to *New York Times* reporter Lucy Tompkins in 2020, "a disproportionately low number of people of color visit national parks."[14] Additionally, according to Dorceta E. Taylor in *The Rise of the American Conservation Movement* (Duke University Press, 2016), many people of color avoid joining the Sierra Club and other organizations whose histories involved pursuing environmental projects that benefitted only white Americans or were based in racial exclusion in other ways. Perhaps Muir's unwillingness to be more inclusive in his writings is partially to blame. Sadly, his vision of preserving the wild involved the expulsion of Native peoples from their homes in Yosemite Valley and elsewhere.

That John Muir's lifelong devotion to wilderness preservation has made a valuable contribution to humanity cannot be denied. However, his racist views must not be overlooked; indeed, they must be factored into his vision of nature. Wilderness preservation, in fact, is inextricable from race: we cannot really regard wild nature as a transcendent realm apart from the Native peoples who have always inhabited those realms. Yet John Muir believed those inhabitants somehow sullied "pristine" nature, and he felt no compunction about their removal.

How This Book Is Organized

Muir defies labeling; and so, in surveying his considerable body of work, one does not find mutually exclusive categories; instead, we can identify phases in which we see one of five sensibilities manifested. Accordingly, I have organized the book's selections in the context of these sensibilities, which I call, in reference to the sequential stages of his life, The Visionary Inventor, The Wandering Minstrel, The Nature Scribe and Rhapsode, The Global Adventurer, and The Planet Steward.

The Visionary Inventor

Because his father forbade him to read novels ("The Deevil's ain buik o' lies!" was Daniel Muir's assessment of a novel[15]), John would get up in the middle of the night to read on the sly, but during the winter months, when a fire was needed, his father would awaken. And so John shifted his attention to an equally joyous pursuit: inventing fanciful yet practical machines such as a plant-growth measurer, an all-in-one barometer-hygrometer-pyrometer, a study desk that automatically rotated his books, and various early-rising machines, including a bed that propped the sleeper upright on the floor at the pre-appointed time. In *The Story of My Boyhood and Youth*, Muir captures the delight of such inventiveness, which proved to be an antidote to the drudgery of farm life and his father's relentlessly harsh rule.

The Wandering Minstrel

Muir's first major excursion into wilderness took place during the Civil War. A committed pacifist, he ventured into the woodlands and marshes of northern Michigan, then crossed the border into Canada, where he remained until 1866, working as a machinist and teacher. Back in the United States, he went to work for a wagon parts manufacturer in Indianapolis. One evening in March 1867, while adjusting a machine belt, he lost his grip on a file, which flew into his right eye, causing temporary blindness in both eyes. The terror, however short-lived, of losing his sight forever motivated him to reassess his priorities, and later that year he boarded a train for Louisville, Kentucky, to fulfill his dream of exploring the wilderness areas of the South. From Louisville he set out on a two-month, thousand-mile walk through Kentucky, Tennessee (via the Cumberland Mountains—"the first real mountains that my foot ever touched or eyes beheld"), across the western tip of North Carolina, then diagonally across northern Georgia, down the Savannah River to the Atlantic (where he boarded a steamship to Florida), and across Florida to Cedar Key on the Gulf Coast. He'd originally planned to sail to South America but fell ill with malaria. After recuperating in Havana, he set sail for San Francisco.

Although the resulting book, *A Thousand-Mile Walk to the Gulf*, published posthumously in 1916, is composed of reworked journal entries (characteristic of most of Muir's books), it still retains much of the spontaneity of those original entries. These writings capture well their author's wanderlust heart. But they also capture, as one of his biographers, Herbert F. Smith, so aptly states, "the narrative of a man who had not yet made up his mind" about the direction his life was to take.[16]

Muir's excursions brought him into contact not only with different geographical regions of the country but also with a diverse group of people, including Native Americans and African Americans. Reading his accounts of these observations and encounters, we learn that his principal interests lay with the land—the mountains, the caves, the trees, the animal life. The human encounters were of secondary interest at best. Although he walked through Georgia just a few years after the end of the Civil War, he focused almost exclusively on the nonhuman world, turning conversations away from politics and social issues to plant and animal life.

THE NATURE SCRIBE AND RHAPSODE

With the wilderness now in his blood, and having read about the sublime, vast mountain wildernesses of the Sierra—especially of the Yosemite Valley—Muir was eager to embark on the path that would enable him to bring his gifts as a naturalist to fruition. Like the great geologist Louis Agassiz, who had first theorized the existence of an ice age and of glaciation, Muir too believed that "a physical fact is as sacred as a moral principle."[17]

On virtually every page of his Sierra books—*The Mountains of California* (1894), *My First Summer in the Sierra* (1911), and *The Yosemite* (1912)—we feel the author's awe at the majesty of mountain wilderness, enhanced rather than diminished by the author's well-trained scientific scrutiny, as in this description of Sierra summit trees from *The Mountains of California*:

> There are two trees in the Sierra forests that are never blown down, so long as they continue in sound health. These are the juniper and the dwarf pine of the summit peaks. Their stiff, crooked roots grip the storm-beaten ledges like eagles' claws, while their lithe, cord-like branches bend round compliantly, offering but slight holds for winds, however violent. The other alpine conifers—the needle pine, mountain pine, two-leaved pine, and hemlock spruce—are never thinned out by this agent to any destructive extent, on account of their growth.[18]

Even Muir's letters often possess the same fusion of reportage and poetic description, as in the two letters to Jeanne Carr that appear in this section. Jeanne Carr, wife of the botanist and Berkeley professor Ezra Carr (with whom Muir had studied when they were both at the University of Wisconsin in the early 1860s), nurtured Muir's botanical and geological studies in the wild and encouraged—prodded—him to publish. "She formed the bridge between the crabbed isolation of his boyhood and the world of men he would have to live in," writes Linnie Marsh Wolfe in her biography of Muir. "By her unfailing tact and faith in his genius she directed his aims and helped fit him for leadership."[19] I venture to add that she was also his muse, inspiring him, as in his "Nut Time" letter, to such eloquent flights of fancy as to make him seem like a jubilant Tom o' Bedlam.

The Global Adventurer

John Muir the adventurer was not too different from John Muir the wanderer or the poet-naturalist or even the inventor-machinist. The distinctions are matters of degree, or of principal sensibility. For example, while in Yosemite, he put his machinist's skills to use in helping to operate a sawmill. He was certainly the adventurer when he rode a snow avalanche down the north slope of Cloud's Rest in Yosemite, or when he perched himself on a lip of rock in order to better experience the sensation of a waterfall—adventures he relates in *The Yosemite*, chapters 1 and 3, respectively. His sensibilities were different in each "incarnation," however. In Wisconsin his focus was to learn and to create labor-saving devices that would free him to study, or enable him to earn more money; on his thousand-mile trek through the South, it was to experience freedom, to discover himself. In California it was to exult in the sublime beauty of the Sierra and to solve the mystery of how Yosemite Valley had formed.

But something else stirred in Muir's blood: a sheer craving for adventure—adventure for its own sake, for the intrinsic life-thrills it provided. It is what his near contemporary, Jack London, would refer to as "the call of the wild."

And so, in 1879, Muir heeded the call of the northern wildernesses of Puget Sound, British Columbia, and especially Alaska, which, although it had already begun to be exploited by whites for its resources, was as close to unexploited wilderness as Muir would ever see in North America. During these Alaska trips Muir also began to pay close attention to the Native peoples and their customs (as in the piece "Eskimos and Walrus").

Soon after marrying Louisa ("Louie") Strentzel in 1880 and beginning a happy, successful family life, Muir embarked on his second Alaska adventure—a glacier-exploration trip that resulted in his most popular book. Accompanied by a little black border collie mutt he named Stickeen (after the Stickeen Indians, or Tahltan people, who had originally adopted him), Muir ventured into Taylor Bay to explore on foot a newly discovered glacier but got trapped. In *Stickeen* (1909), first published in the *Overland Monthly* magazine as "An Adventure with a Dog and a Glacier," Muir demonstrates his exceptional storytelling ability. Also, in a mysterious way, his intrepid companion seems to embody all that Muir himself represented. As publisher Malcolm Margolin explains in his afterword to the illustrated Heyday edition of the story, "It was as if the dog—driven to its utmost limits that day on the glacier—became momentarily transparent; and when Muir looked through to the essence of its being, what he saw in Stickeen was not very different from what he saw in himself."

THE PLANET STEWARD

One might argue that anyone who reveres the natural world in all of its manifestations, as did John Muir from his earliest romps in the fields of his native Scotland, is well on the way toward becoming an environmentalist. After all, one never has to look very far to find evidence of nature being ravaged. Muir had also long been keenly aware of humanity's role in environmental destruction from having read George Perkins Marsh's *Man and Nature* (1864), a revolutionary and unprecedented investigation of human environmental destruction since ancient times. Marsh asserts:

Man is everywhere a disturbing agent. Wherever he plants his foot, the harmonies of nature are turned to discords. The proportions and accommodations which insured the stability of existing arrangements are overthrown. Indigenous vegetable and animal species are extirpated, and supplanted by others of foreign origin, spontaneous production is forbidden or restricted, and the face of the earth is either laid bare or covered with a new and reluctant growth of vegetable forms, and with alien tribes of animal life.... The fact that, of all organic beings, man alone is to be regarded as essentially a destructive power ... tends to prove that, though living in physical nature, he is not of her.[20]

One cannot help but suspect that Muir, after reading the above passage, felt compelled to prove Marsh right. Indeed, Muir's environmentalism was grounded in the notion that the natural world not only transcended humanity but needed to be preserved from exploitation by land developers and industrialists.

In 1876, after sojourning among the giant sequoias and observing their rapid decimation, he published the newspaper article "God's First Temples: How Shall We Preserve Our Forests?" This powerful piece, which appeared in the *Sacramento Daily Record-Union* (Feb. 5, 1876), gave the public a vivid overview of forest destruction and advanced the case for federal protection. But it wasn't until 1889 that Muir turned his attention full time to the rapidly developing environmental crises in California. After surveying the destruction in Yosemite with Robert Underwood Johnson (an editor at *Century Magazine*), the two men decided to make the case for federal protection of the area, to advocate making it a national park. Johnson would lobby in Washington, D.C.; Muir would write articles for *Century*. Their plan worked and, in the fall of 1889 Congress passed a bill to make Yosemite a national park (the nation's third), effective the following year. Over the next decade, more forest reserves were created across the nation.

John Muir and the Sierra Club

Even before precious public lands became national parks, it was clear that an organization was needed to protect them from privatization and exploitation by land developers. Since the 1860s organizations had sprouted up around the country, such as the Alpine Club in Massachusetts, the Rocky Mountain Club in Colorado Springs, and various Audubon Society clubs, all of which aimed to maintain wilderness areas for specific recreational purposes like mountain climbing and birding. According to environmentalist and historian Tom Turner, two professors from the University of California, Berkeley, J. H. Senger and William Dallman Armes, set up a founding meeting for a new association that would work to protect Yosemite and Yellowstone and encourage recreational activities in these parks. "Muir responded enthusiastically" to the plan, Turner writes, quoting Muir, who said he was "hoping that we will be able to do something for wildness and make the mountains glad."[21] In September 1892 the Sierra Club was founded and Muir was unanimously elected its first president—a position he retained until his death.

In 2020, the Sierra Club had a reckoning with a concept that underscored its founding: the idea of nature's "purity," a notion that was entwined with those of white supremacy, which included the assumption held by Muir and others that the Native peoples inhabiting these wilderness areas detracted from their beauty and purity. The Sierra Club has acknowledged that Muir's racist, white supremacist views were interwoven with the organization's founding principles.

John Muir scrutinized and celebrated wild nature on behalf of the human soul as he understood it more than one hundred years ago. Can he still speak to us today? Yes, but we must reconsider his legacy even though "the world is too much with us," as Wordsworth lamented two hundred years ago in a famous sonnet that starts with those words and later includes the line "Little we see in Nature that is ours." Muir can teach us once again to see what is ours—and *not* ours—in the natural world. By reading his best and worst together, we can also learn how the wider conservation movement and American nature writing have excluded non-white perspectives, even from those who have and continue to live deeply in relationship to the natural world, California Indians among them. We must know all of Muir: the mystic, the scientist, the ardent activist and adventurer, and the man unable to shake his prejudices. Even more, knowing him better, we can work to repair the damage done to those whose voices and lives meant little to Muir. More than a century later, greater numbers of us can come to understand that the American wilderness was never empty, was never even really wild. Yet even still, we take heart and inspiration from him at his best: "Go now and then for fresh life," he wrote in his journal on the way to the Yosemite Valley in September 1874. "[Even] if most of humanity must go through this down stage of development—just as divers hold their breath and come ever and anon to the surface to breathe . . . go to the snow-flowers in winter, to the sun-flowers in summer. . . . Go up and away for life."[22] He is not merely telling us to jump into our RVs and spend a weekend in the mountains; he is reminding us that, like Antaeus, we cannot remain uprooted from the earth for too long without losing our sense of what it means to be fully alive. How we restore that relationship for everyone is the challenge that faces us all today as the inheritors of Muir's legacy.

SELECTIONS NEW TO THIS EDITION

The following selections have been added to those from the original edition to provide a more comprehensive picture of John Muir's ideas and experiences, including his views of people of color—particularly African Americans and the Native peoples he encountered in the Sierra and in Alaska:

"Kentucky Forests and Caves" and "Through Florida's Swamps and Forests," from *A Thousand-Mile Walk to the Gulf*

"In Camp on the North Fork of the Merced" and "The Mono Indians of Bloody Canon," from *A Near View of the High Sierras*

"A Yosemite Earthquake," from *The Yosemite*

Notes

1 *The Yosemite* (New York: Anchor Books, 1912), 66.

2 An evangelical, utopian sect founded in America by the Scotsman Alexander Campbell. Unlike Calvinism, and more in keeping with the spirit of American democracy and liberty, it held that salvation was available to anyone, not just to a pre-ordained "Elect."

3 Ralph Waldo Emerson, "Address to the Harvard Divinity School Seniors," July 15, 1838, in *Selections from Ralph Waldo Emerson*, ed. Stephen E. Whicher (Boston: Houghton-Mifflin Co., 1957), 113.

4 Robert Underwood Johnson, "John Muir As I Knew Him," *Sierra Club Bulletin*, January 1916, Web.

5 Journal entry from January 18, 1869, in *John of the Mountains: Unpublished Journals of John Muir* (Madison: University of Wisconsin Press, 1979).

6 *The Story of My Boyhood and Youth* (Boston: Houghton Mifflin, 1913), 178–179.

7 *The Life and Letters of John Muir*, ed. William Frederick Badè (Boston and New York: Houghton Mifflin, 1924), I:20–22.

8 *The Story of My Boyhood and Youth*, 93.

9 Ibid, 89.

10 *John of the Mountains*, 95.

11 Marion Randall Parsons, "John Muir and the Alaska Book," in *John Muir: His Life and Letters and Other Writings*, ed. Terry Gifford (London: Baton Wicks, 1996), 884.

12 *The Life and Letters of John Muir*, I:300.

13 See, for example, Mark David Spencer, *Dispossessing the Wilderness: Indian Removal and the Making of National Parks* (New York: Oxford University Press, 1999).

14 Lucy Tompkins, "Sierra Club Says It Must Confront Its Founder's Racism," *New York Times*, July 24, 2020, A14.

15 Quoted by Linnie Marsh Wolfe, *Son of the Wilderness: The Life of John Muir* (New York: A. A. Knopf, 1945), 46.

16 Herbert F. Smith, *John Muir* (New York: Twayne, 1965), 35.

17 Agassiz in conversation with his pupils, with whom he traveled to Lake Superior in 1848; quoted by Linnie Marsh Wolfe, *Son of the Wilderness*, 76.

18 *The Mountains of California* (New York: The Century Co., 1894), 246.

19 *Son of the Wilderness*, 79.

20 George Perkins Marsh, *Man and Nature* (London: S. Low, Son and Marston, 1864), 36–37.

21 Tom Turner, *Sierra Club: 100 Years of Protecting Nature* (New York: Harry N. Abrams, Inc., 1991), 48.

22 *John of the Mountains*, 191.

PART ONE:

The Visionary Inventor

Knowledge and Inventions

Several of our neighbors had brought a dozen or two of all sorts of books, which I borrowed and read, keeping all of them except the religious ones carefully hidden from Father's eye. Among these were Scott's novels, which, like all other novels, were strictly forbidden but devoured with glorious pleasure in secret. Father was easily persuaded to buy Josephus' *Wars of the Jews*, and d'Aubigné's *History of the Reformation*, and I tried hard to get him to buy Plutarch's *Lives*, which, as I told him, everybody, even religious people, praised as a grand good book; but he would have nothing to do with the old pagan until the graham bread and anti-flesh doctrines came suddenly into our backwoods neighborhood, making a stir something like phrenology and spirit-rappings, which were as mysterious in their attacks as influenza. He then thought it possible that Plutarch might be turned to account on the food question by revealing what those old Greeks and Romans ate to make them strong; and so at last we gained our glorious Plutarch. Dick's *Christian Philosopher*, which I borrowed from a neighbor, I thought I might venture to read in the open, trusting that the word "Christian" would be proof against its cautious condemnation. But Father balked at the word "philosopher," and quoted from the Bible a verse that spoke of "philosophy falsely so-called." I then ventured to speak in defense of the book, arguing that we could not do without at least a little of the most useful kinds of philosophy.

"Yes, we can," he said with enthusiasm. "The Bible is the only book human beings can possibly require throughout all the journey from earth to heaven."

"But how," I contended, "can we find the way to heaven without the Bible, and how after we grow old can we read the Bible without a little helpful science? Just think, Father, you cannot read your Bible without spectacles, and millions of others are in the same fix; and spectacles cannot be made without some knowledge of the science of optics."

"Oh!" he replied, perceiving the drift of the argument. "There will always be plenty of worldly people to make spectacles."

To this I stubbornly replied with a quotation from the Bible with reference to the time coming when "all shall know the Lord from the least even to the greatest," and then who will make the spectacles? But he still objected to my reading that book, called me a contumacious quibbler too fond of disputation, and ordered me to return it to the accommodating owner. I managed, however, to read it later.

On the food question, Father insisted that those who argued for a vegetable diet were in the right, because our teeth showed plainly that they were made with reference to fruit and grain and not for flesh like those of dogs and wolves and tigers. He therefore promptly adopted a vegetable diet and requested mother to make the bread from graham flour instead of bolted flour. Mother put both kinds on the table, and meat also, to let all the family take their choice, and while Father was insisting on the foolishness of eating flesh, I came to her help by calling Father's attention to the passage in the Bible which told the story of Elijah the prophet who, when he was pursued by enemies who wanted to take his life, was hidden by the Lord by the brook Cherith, and fed by ravens; and surely the Lord knew what was good to eat, whether bread or meat. And on what, I asked, did the Lord feed Elijah? On vegetables or graham bread? No, he directed the ravens to feed his prophet on flesh. The Bible being the sole rule, Father at once acknowledged that he was mistaken. The Lord never would have sent flesh to Elijah by the ravens if graham bread were better.

I remember as a great and sudden discovery that the poetry of the Bible, Shakespeare, and Milton was a source of inspiring, exhilarating, uplifting pleasure; and I became anxious to know all the poets and saved up small sums to buy as many of their books as possible. Within three or four years I was the proud possessor of parts of Shakespeare's, Milton's, Cowper's, Henry Kirke White's,

Campbell's, and Akenside's works, and quite a number of others seldom read nowadays. I think it was in my fifteenth year that I began to relish good literature with enthusiasm, and smack my lips over favorite lines, but there was desperately little time for reading, even in the winter evenings—only a few stolen minutes now and then. Father's strict rule was, straight to bed immediately after family worship, which in winter was usually over by eight o'clock. I was in the habit of lingering in the kitchen with a book and candle after the rest of the family had retired, and considered myself fortunate if I got five minutes' reading before Father noticed the light and ordered me to bed; an order that, of course, I immediately obeyed. But night after night I tried to steal minutes in the same lingering way, and how keenly precious those minutes were, few nowadays can know. Father failed perhaps two or three times in a whole winter to notice my light for nearly ten minutes, magnificent golden blocks of time, long to be remembered like holidays or geological periods. One evening when I was reading Church history, Father was particularly irritable and called out with hope-killing emphasis, "John, go to bed! Must I give you a separate order every night to get you to go to bed? Now, I will have no irregularity in the family; you must go when the rest go, and without my having to tell you." Then, as an afterthought, as if judging that his words and tone of voice were too severe for so pardonable an offense as reading a religious book, he unwarily added: "If you will read, get up in the morning and read. You may get up in the morning as early as you like."

That night I went to bed wishing with all my heart and soul that somebody or something might call me out of sleep to avail myself of this wonderful indulgence, and next morning to my joyful surprise I awoke before Father called me. A boy sleeps soundly after working all day in the snowy woods, but that frosty morning I sprang out of bed as if called by a trumpet blast, rushed downstairs, scarce feeling my chilblains, enormously eager to see how much time I had won; and when I held up my candle to a little clock that stood on a bracket in the kitchen I found that it was only one o'clock. I had gained five hours, almost half a day! "Five hours to myself!" I said, "five huge, solid hours!" I can hardly think of any other event in my life, any discovery I ever made that gave birth to joy so transportingly glorious as the possession of these five frosty hours.

In the glad, tumultuous excitement of so much suddenly acquired time-wealth, I hardly knew what to do with it. I first thought of going on with my reading, but the zero weather would make a fire necessary, and it occurred to me that Father might object to the cost of firewood that took time to chop. Therefore, I prudently decided to go down cellar and begin work on a model of a self-setting sawmill I had invented. Next morning I managed to get up at the same gloriously early hour, and though the temperature of the cellar was a little below the freezing point, and my light was only a tallow candle, the mill work went joyfully on. There were a few tools in a corner of the cellar—a vise, files, a hammer, chisels, etc., that Father had brought from Scotland, but no saw excepting a coarse, crooked one that was unfit for sawing dry hickory or oak. So I made a fine-tooth saw suitable for my work out of a strip of steel that had formed part of an old-fashioned corset, which cut the hardest wood smoothly. I also made my own bradawls, punches, and a pair of compasses, out of wire and old files.

My workshop was immediately under Father's bed, and the filing and tapping in making cogwheels, journals, cams, etc., must, no doubt, have annoyed him, but with the permission he had granted in his mind, and doubtless hoping that I would soon tire of getting up at one o'clock, he impatiently waited about two weeks before saying a word. I did not vary more than five minutes from one o'clock all winter, nor did I feel any bad effects whatever, nor did I think at all about the subject as to whether so little sleep might be in any way injurious; it was a grand triumph of willpower over cold and common comfort and work-weariness in abruptly cutting down my ten hours' allowance of sleep to five. I simply felt that I was rich beyond anything I could have dreamed of or hoped for. I was far more than happy. Like Tam O'Shanter I was glorious, "O'er a' the ills o' life victorious."

Father, as was customary in Scotland, gave thanks and asked a blessing before meals, not merely as a matter of form and decent Christian manners, for he regarded food as a gift derived directly from the hands of the Father in heaven. Therefore, every meal to him was a sacrament requiring conduct and attitude of mind not unlike that befitting the Lord's Supper. No idle word was allowed to be spoken at our table, much less any laughing or fun or story-telling. When we were at the breakfast table, about two weeks after the great golden time discovery, Father cleared his throat prelimi-nary, as we all knew, to saying something considered important. I feared that it was to be on the subject of my early rising and dreaded the withdrawal of the permission he had granted on account of the noise I made, but still hoped that, as he had given his word that I might get up as early as I wished, he would as a Scotchman stand to it, even though it was given in an unguarded moment and taken in a sense unreasonably far-reaching. The solemn sacramental silence was broken by the dreaded question:

"John, what time is it when you get up in the morning?"

"About one o'clock," I replied in a low, meek, guilty tone of voice.

"And what kind of a time is that, getting up in the middle of the night and disturbing the whole family?"

I simply reminded him of the permission he had freely granted me to get up as early as I wished.

"I know it," he said in an almost agonized tone of voice. "I know I gave you that miserable permission, but I never imagined that you would get up in the middle of the night."

To this I cautiously made no reply, but continued to listen for the heavenly one o'clock call, and it never failed.

After completing my self-setting sawmill I dammed one of the streams in the meadow and put the mill in operation. This inven-tion was speedily followed by a lot of others—waterwheels, curious door locks and latches, thermometers, hygrometers, pyrometers, clocks, a barometer, an automatic contrivance for feeding the horses at any required hour, a lamplighter and fire-lighter, an early-or-late-rising machine, and so forth.

After the sawmill was proved and discharged from my mind, I happened to think it would be a fine thing to make a timekeeper which would tell the day of the week and the day of the month, as well as strike like a common clock and point out the hours; also to have an attachment whereby it could be connected with a bedstead to set me on my feet at any hour in the morning; also to start fires, light lamps, etc. I had learned the time laws of the pendulum from a book, but with this exception I knew nothing of timekeepers, for I had never seen the inside of any sort of clock or watch. After long brooding, the novel clock was at length completed in my mind, and was tried and found to be durable and to work well and look well before I had begun to build it in wood. I carried small parts of it in my pocket to whittle at when I was out at work on the farm, using every spare or stolen moment within reach without Father's knowing anything about it. In the middle of summer, when harvesting was in progress, the novel time machine was nearly completed. It was hidden upstairs in a spare bedroom where some tools were kept. I did the making and mending on the farm, but one day at noon, when I happened to be away, Father went upstairs for a hammer or something and discovered the mysterious machine back of the bedstead. My sister Margaret saw him on his knees examining it, and at the first opportunity whispered in my ear, "John, Father saw that thing you're making upstairs." None of the family knew what I was doing, but they knew very well that all such work was frowned on by Father and kindly warned me of any danger that threatened my plans. The fine invention seemed doomed to destruction before its time-ticking commenced, though I thought it handsome, had so long carried it in my mind, and like the nest of Burns's wee mousie, it had cost me many a weary whittling nibble. When we were at dinner several days after the sad discovery, Father began to clear his throat to speak, and I feared the doom of martyrdom was about to be pronounced on my grand clock.

"John," he inquired, "what is that thing you are making upstairs?"

I replied in desperation that I didn't know what to call it.

"What! You mean to say you don't know what you are trying to do?"

"Oh, yes," I said, "I know very well what I am doing."

"What, then, is the thing for?"

"It's for a lot of things," I replied, "but getting people up early in the morning is one of the main things it is intended for; therefore, it might perhaps be called an early-rising machine."

After getting up so extravagantly early all the last memorable winter, to make a machine for getting up perhaps still earlier seemed so ridiculous that he very nearly laughed. But after controlling himself and getting command of a sufficiently solemn face and voice he said severely, "Do you not think it is very wrong to waste your time on such nonsense?"

"No," I said meekly. "I don't think I'm doing any wrong."

"Well," he replied, "I assure you I do, and if you were only half as zealous in the study of religion as you are in contriving and whittling these useless, nonsensical things, it would be infinitely better for you. I want you to be like Paul, who said that he desired to know nothing among men but Christ and Him crucified."

To this I made no reply, gloomily believing my fine machine was to be burned but still taking what comfort I could in realizing that anyhow I had enjoyed inventing and making it.

After a few days, finding that nothing more was to be said and that Father after all had not had the heart to destroy it, all necessity for secrecy being ended, I finished it in the half-hours that we had at noon and set it in the parlor between two chairs, hung moraine boulders that had come from the direction of Lake Superior on it for weights, and set it running. We were then hauling grain into the barn. Father at this period devoted himself entirely to the Bible and did no farm work whatever. The clock had a good loud tick, and when he heard it strike, one of my sisters told me that he left his study, went to the parlor, got down on his knees and carefully examined the machinery, which was all in plain sight, not being enclosed in a case. This he did repeatedly, and evidently seemed a little proud of my ability to invent and whittle such a thing, though careful to give no encouragement for anything more of the kind in future.

The World and the University

When I told Father that I was about to leave home and inquired whether, if I should happen to be in need of money, he would send me a little, he said, "No; depend entirely on yourself." Good advice, I suppose, but surely needlessly severe for a bashful, home-loving boy who had worked so hard. I had the gold sovereign that my grandfather had given me when I left Scotland, and a few dollars, perhaps ten, that I had made by raising a few bushels of grain on a little patch of sandy, abandoned ground. So when I left home to try the world, I had only about fifteen dollars in my pocket.

Strange to say, Father carefully taught us to consider ourselves very poor worms of the dust, conceived in sin, etc., and devoutly believed that quenching every spark of pride and self-confidence was a sacred duty, without realizing that in so doing he might at the same time be quenching everything else. Praise he considered most venomous, and tried to assure me that when I was fairly out in the wicked world making my own way I would soon learn that although I might have thought him a hard taskmaster at times, strangers were far harder. On the contrary, I found no lack of kindness and sympathy. All the baggage I carried was a package made up of the two clocks and a small thermometer made of a piece of old washboard, all three tied together, with no covering or case of any sort, the whole looking like one very complicated machine.

The aching parting from mother and my sisters was, of course, hard to bear. Father let David drive me down to Pardeeville, a place I had never before seen, though it was only nine miles south of the Hickory Hill home. When we arrived at the village tavern, it seemed deserted. Not a single person was in sight. I set my clock baggage on the rickety platform. David said good-bye and started for home, leaving me alone in the world. The grinding noise made by the wagon in turning short brought out the landlord, and the first thing that caught his eye was my strange bundle. Then he looked at me and said, "Hello, young man, what's this?"

"Machines," I said, "for keeping time and getting up in the morning, and so forth."

"Well! Well! That's a mighty queer getup. You must be a down-east Yankee. Where did you get the pattern for such a thing?"

"In my head," I said.

Someone down the street happened to notice the landlord looking intently at something and came up to see what it was. Three or four people in that little village formed an attractive crowd, and in fifteen or twenty minutes the greater part of the population of Pardeeville stood gazing in a circle around my strange hickory belongings. I kept outside of the circle to avoid being seen and had the advantage of hearing the remarks without being embarrassed. Almost everyone as he came up would say, "What's that? What's it for? Who made it?" The landlord would answer them all alike, "Why, a young man that lives out in the country somewhere made it, and he says it's a thing for keeping time, getting up in the morning, and something that I didn't understand. I don't know what he meant." "Oh, no!" one of the crowd would say, "that can't be. It's for something else—something mysterious. Mark my words, you'll see all about it in the newspapers some of these days." A curious little fellow came running up the street, joined the crowd, stood on tiptoe to get sight of the wonder, quickly made up his mind, and shouted in crisp, confident, cock-crowing style, "I know what that contraption's for. It's a machine for taking the bones out of fish."

This was in the time of the great popular phrenology craze, when the fences and barns along the roads throughout the country were plastered with big skull-bump posters, headed, "Know Thyself," and advising everybody to attend schoolhouse lectures to have their heads explained and be told what they were good for and whom they ought to marry. My mechanical bundle seemed to bring a good deal of this phrenology to mind, for many of the onlookers would say, "I wish I could see that boy's head—he must have a tremendous bump of invention." Others complimented me by saying, "I wish I had that fellow's head. I'd rather have it than the best farm in the state."

I stayed overnight at this little tavern, waiting for a train. In the morning I went to the station and set my bundle on the platform. Along came the thundering train, a glorious sight, the first train I had ever waited for. When the conductor saw my queer baggage, he cried, "Hello! What have we here?"

"Inventions for keeping time, early rising, and so forth. May I take them into the car with me?"

"You can take them where you like," he replied, "but you had better give them to the baggage-master. If you take them into the car they will draw a crowd and might get broken."

So I gave them to the baggage-master and made haste to ask the conductor whether I might ride on the engine. He good-naturedly said, "Yes, it's the right place for you. Run ahead, and tell the engineer what I say." But the engineer bluntly refused to let me on, saying, "It don't matter what the conductor told you. I say you can't ride on my engine."

By this time the conductor, standing ready to start his train, was watching to see what luck I had, and when he saw me returning came ahead to meet me.

"The engineer won't let me on," I reported.

"Won't he?" said the kind conductor. "Oh! I guess he will. You come down with me." And so he actually took the time and patience to walk the length of that long train to get me onto the engine.

"Charlie," said he, addressing the engineer, "don't you ever take a passenger?"

"Very seldom," he replied.

"Anyhow, I wish you would take this young man on. He has the strangest machines in the baggage car I ever saw in my life. I believe he could make a locomotive. He wants to see the engine running. Let him on." Then in a low whisper, he told me to jump on, which I did gladly, the engineer offering neither encouragement nor objection.

As soon as the train was started, the engineer asked what the "strange thing" the conductor spoke of really was.

"Only inventions for keeping time, getting folk up in the morning, and so forth," I hastily replied, and before he could ask any more questions I asked permission to go outside of the cab to see the machinery. This he kindly granted, adding, "Be careful not to fall off, and when you hear me whistling for a station you come back, because if it is reported against me to the superintendent that I allow boys to run all over my engine, I might lose my job."

Assuring him that I would come back promptly, I went out and walked along the footboard on the side of the boiler, watching the magnificent machine rushing through the landscapes as if glorying in its strength like a living creature. While seated on the cowcatcher platform, I seemed to be fairly flying, and the wonderful display of power and motion was enchanting. This was the first time I had ever been on a train, much less a locomotive, since I had left Scotland. When I got to Madison, I thanked the kind conductor and engineer for my glorious ride, inquired the way to the Fair, shouldered my inventions, and walked to the fairground.

When I applied for an admission ticket at a window by the gate I told the agent that I had something to exhibit.

"What is it?" he inquired.

"Well, here it is. Look at it."

When he craned his neck through the window and got a glimpse of my bundle, he cried excitedly, "Oh! You don't need a ticket. Come right in."

When I inquired of the agent where such things as mine should be exhibited, he said, "You see that building up on the hill with a big flag on it? That's the Fine Arts Hall, and it's just the place for your wonderful invention."

So I went up to the Fine Arts Hall and looked in, wondering if they would allow wooden things in so fine a place.

I was met at the door by a dignified gentleman, who greeted me kindly and said, "Young man, what have we got here?"

"Two clocks and a thermometer," I replied.

"Did you make these? They look wonderfully beautiful and novel and must, I think, prove the most interesting feature of the fair."

"Where shall I place them?" I inquired.

"Just look around, young man, and choose the place you like best, whether it is occupied or not. You can have your pick of all the building, and a carpenter to make the necessary shelving and assist you every way possible!"

So I quickly had a shelf made large enough for all of them, went out on the hill and picked up some glacial boulders of the right size for weights, and in fifteen or twenty minutes the clocks were running. They seemed to attract more attention than anything else in the Hall. I got lots of praise from the crowd and the newspaper reporters. The local press reports were copied into the eastern papers. It was considered wonderful that a boy on a farm had been able to invent and make such things, and almost every spectator foretold good fortune. But I had been so lectured by my father above all things to avoid praise that I was afraid to read those kind newspaper notices and never clipped out or preserved any of them, just glanced at them and turned away my eyes from beholding vanity. They gave me a prize of ten or fifteen dollars and a diploma for wonderful things not down in the list of exhibits.

Many years later, after I had written articles and books, I received a letter from the gentleman who had charge of the Fine Arts Hall. He proved to be the professor of English literature in the University of Wisconsin at this fair time, and long afterward he sent me clippings of reports of his lectures. He had a lecture on me, discussing style, etcetera, and telling how well he remembered my arrival at the Hall in my shirtsleeves with those mechanical wonders on my shoulder, and so forth, and so forth. These inventions, though of little importance, opened all doors for me and made marks that have lasted many years, simply, I suppose, because they were original and promising.

I was looking around in the mean time to find out where I should go to seek my fortune. An inventor at the fair, by the name of Wiard, was exhibiting an iceboat he had invented to run on the upper Mississippi from Prairie du Chien to St. Paul during the winter months, explaining how useful it would be thus to make a highway of the river while it was closed to ordinary navigation by ice. After he saw my inventions, he offered me a place in his foundry and machine shop in Prairie du Chien and promised to assist me all he could. So I made up my mind to accept his offer and rode with him to Prairie du Chien in his iceboat, which was mounted on a flat car. I soon found, however, that he was seldom at home and that I was not likely to learn much at his small shop. I found a place where I could work for my board and devote my spare hours to mechanical drawing, geometry, and physics, making but little headway, however, although the Pelton family, for whom I worked, were very kind. I made up my mind after a few months' stay in Prairie du Chien to return to Madison, hoping that in some way I might be able to gain an education.

At Madison I raised a few dollars by making and selling a few of those bedsteads that set the sleepers on their feet in the morning— inserting in the footboard the works of an ordinary clock that could be bought for a dollar. I also made a few dollars addressing circulars in an insurance office, while at the same time I was paying my board by taking care of a pair of horses and going errands. This is of no great interest except that I was thus winning my bread while hoping that something would turn up that might enable me to make money enough to enter the State University. This was my ambition, and it never wavered no matter what I was doing. No university, it seemed to me, could be more admirably situated, and as I sauntered about it, charmed with its fine lawns and trees and beautiful lakes, and saw the students going and coming with their books, and occasionally practicing with a theodolite in measuring distances, I thought that if I could only join them it would be the greatest joy of life. I was desperately hungry and thirsty for knowledge and willing to endure anything to get it.

One day I chanced to meet a student who had noticed my inventions at the fair and now recognized me. And when I said, "You are fortunate fellows to be allowed to study in this beautiful place. I wish I could join you," he asked, "Well, why don't you?" "I haven't money enough," I said. "Oh, as to money," he reassuringly explained, "very little is required. I presume you're able to enter the Freshman class, and you can board yourself as quite a number of us do at a cost of about a dollar a week. The baker and milkman come every day. You can live on bread and milk." Well, I thought, maybe

I have money enough for at least one beginning term. Anyhow I couldn't help trying.

With fear and trembling, overladen with ignorance, I called on Professor Stirling, the Dean of the Faculty, who was then Acting President, presented my case, and told him how far I had got on with my studies at home, and that I hadn't been to school since leaving Scotland at the age of eleven years, excepting one short term of a couple of months at a district school, because I could not be spared from the farm work. After hearing my story, the kind professor welcomed me to the glorious University—next, it seemed to me, to the Kingdom of Heaven. After a few weeks in the preparatory department, I entered the Freshman class. In Latin, I found that one of the books in use I had already studied in Scotland. So, after an interruption of a dozen years, I began my Latin over again where I had left off; and strange to say, most of it came back to me, especially the grammar which I had committed to memory at the Dunbar Grammar School.

During the four years that I was in the University, I earned enough in the harvest fields during the long summer vacations to carry me through the balance of each year, working very hard, cutting with a cradle four acres of wheat a day, and helping to put it in the shock. But, having to buy books and paying, I think, thirty-two dollars a year for instruction, and occasionally buying acids and retorts, glass tubing, bell-glasses, flasks, etc., I had to cut down expenses for board now and then to half a dollar a week.

One winter I taught school ten miles north of Madison, earning much-needed money at the rate of twenty dollars a month, "boarding 'round," and keeping up my University work by studying at night. As I was not then well enough off to own a watch, I used one of my hickory clocks, not only for keeping time, but for starting the school fire in the cold mornings, and regulating class times. I carried it out on my shoulder to the old log schoolhouse, and set it to work on a little shelf nailed to one of the knotty, bulging logs. The winter was very cold, and I had to go to the schoolhouse and start the fire about eight o'clock to warm it before the arrival of the scholars. This was a rather trying job, and one that my clock might easily be made to do. Therefore, after supper one evening I told the head of the family with whom I was boarding that if he would give me a candle I would go back to the schoolhouse and make arrangements for lighting the fire at eight o'clock, without my having to be present until time to open the school at nine. He said, "Oh! Young man, you have some curious things in the school room, but I don't think you can do that." I said, "Oh, yes! It's easy," and in hardly more than an hour, the simple job was completed. I had only to place a teaspoonful of powdered chlorate of potash and sugar on the stove-hearth near a few shavings and kindling, and at the required time make the clock, through a simple arrangement, touch the inflammable mixture with a drop of sulphuric acid. Every evening after school was dismissed, I shoveled out what was left of the fire into the snow, put in a little kindling, filled up the big box stove with heavy oak wood, placed the lighting arrangement on the hearth, and set the clock to drop the acid at the hour of eight; all of this requiring only a few minutes.

The first morning after I had made this simple arrangement, I invited the doubting farmer to watch the old squat schoolhouse from a window that overlooked it, to see if a good smoke did not rise from the stovepipe. Sure enough, on the minute, he saw a tall column curling gracefully up through the frosty air, but instead of congratulating me on my success he solemnly shook his head and said in a hollow, lugubrious voice, "Young man, you will be setting fire to the schoolhouse." All winter long that faithful clock fire never failed, and by the time I got to the schoolhouse the stove was usually red-hot.

At the beginning of the long summer vacations I returned to the Hickory Hill farm to earn the means in the harvest-fields to continue my University course, walking all the way to save railroad fares. And although I cradled four acres of wheat a day, I made the long, hard, sweaty day's work still longer and harder by keeping up my study of plants. At the noon hour I collected a large handful, put them in water to keep them fresh, and after supper got to work on them and sat up till after midnight, analyzing and classifying, thus leaving only four hours for sleep; and by the end of the first year, after taking up botany, I knew the principal flowering plants of the region.

I received my first lesson in botany from a student by the name of Griswold, who is now County Judge of the County of Waukesha, Wisconsin. In the university, he was often laughed at on account of his anxiety to instruct others and his frequently saying with fine emphasis, "Imparting instruction is my greatest enjoyment." One memorable day in June, when I was standing on the stone steps of the north dormitory, Mr. Griswold joined me and at once began to teach. He reached up, plucked a flower from an overspreading branch of a locust tree and, handing it to me, said, "Muir, do you know what family this tree belongs to?"

"No," I said, "I don't know anything about botany."

"Well, no matter," said he, "what is it like?"

"It's like a pea flower," I replied.

"That's right. You're right," he said. "It belongs to the pea family."

"But how can that be," I objected, "when the pea is a weak, clinging, straggling herb, and the locust a big, thorny hardwood tree?"

"Yes, that is true," he replied, "as to the difference in size, but it is also true that in all their essential characters they are alike, and therefore they must belong to one and the same family. Just look at the peculiar form of the locust flower; you see that the upper petal, called the banner, is broad and erect, and so is the upper petal of the pea flower. The two lower petals, called the wings, are outspread and wing-shaped; so are those of the pea. And the two petals below the wings are united on their edges, curve upward, and form what is called the keel, and so you see are the corresponding petals of the pea flower. And now look at the stamens and pistils. You see that nine of the ten stamens have their filaments united into a sheath around the pistil, but the tenth stamen has its filament free. These are very marked characters, are they not? And, strange to say, you will find them the same in the tree and in the vine. Now look at the ovules or seeds of the locust, and you will see that they are arranged in a pod or legume like those of the pea. And look at the leaves. You see the leaf of the locust is made up of several leaflets, and so also is the leaf of the pea. Now taste the locust leaf."

I did so and found that it tasted like the leaf of the pea. Nature has used the same seasoning for both, though one is a straggling vine, the other a big tree.

"Now, surely you cannot imagine that all these similar characters are mere coincidences. Do they not rather go to show that the Creator in making the pea vine and locust tree had the same idea in mind, and that plants are not classified arbitrarily? Man has nothing to do with their classification. Nature has attended to all that, giving essential unity with boundless variety, so that the botanist has only to examine plants to learn the harmony of their relations."

This fine lesson charmed me and sent me flying to the woods and meadows in wild enthusiasm. Like everybody else I was always fond of flowers, attracted by their external beauty and purity. Now my eyes were opened to their inner beauty, all alike revealing glorious traces of the thoughts of God, and leading on and on into the infinite cosmos. I wandered away at every opportunity, making long excursions round the lakes, gathering specimens, and keeping them fresh in a bucket in my room to study at night after my regular class tasks were learned, for my eyes never closed on the plant glory I had seen.

Nevertheless, I still indulged my love of mechanical inventions. I invented a desk in which the books I had to study were arranged in order at the beginning of each term. I also made a bed that set me on my feet every morning at the hour determined on, and in dark winter mornings just as the bed set me on the floor it lighted a lamp. Then, after the minutes allowed for dressing had elapsed, a click was heard and the first book to be studied was pushed up from a rack below the top of the desk, thrown open, and allowed to remain there the number of minutes required. Then the machinery closed the book and allowed it to drop back into its stall, then moved the rack forward and threw up the next in order, and so on, all the day being divided according to the times of recitation, and time required and allotted to each study. Besides this, I thought it would be a fine thing in the summertime when the sun rose early, to dispense with the clock-controlled bed machinery and make use of sunbeams instead. This I did simply by taking a lens out of my small spyglass, fixing it on a frame on the sill of my bedroom window, and pointing it to the sunrise; the sunbeams focused on a thread burned it through, allowing the bed machinery to put me on my feet. When I wished to arise at any given time after sunrise, I had only to turn the pivoted frame that held the lens the requisite number of degrees or minutes. Thus I took Emerson's advice and hitched my dumping-wagon bed to a star.

I also invented a machine to make visible the growth of plants and the action of the sunlight, a very delicate contrivance, enclosed in glass. Besides this I invented a barometer and a lot of novel scientific apparatus. My room was regarded as a sort of show place by the professors, who oftentimes brought visitors to it on Saturdays and holidays. And when, some eighteen years after I had left the University, I was sauntering over the campus in time of vacation, and spoke to a man who seemed to be taking some charge of the grounds, he informed me that he was the janitor; and when I inquired what had become of Pat, the janitor in my time and a favorite with the students, he replied that Pat was still alive and well, but now too old to do much work. And when I pointed to the dormitory room that I long ago occupied, he said: "Oh! Then I know who you are," and mentioned my name. "How comes it that you know my name?" I inquired. He explained that "Pat always pointed out that room to newcomers and told long stories about the wonders that used to be in it." So long had the memory of my little inventions survived.

Although I was four years at the University, I did not take the regular course of studies, but instead picked out what I thought would be most useful to me, particularly chemistry, which opened a new world, and mathematics and physics, a little Greek and Latin, botany and geology. I was far from satisfied with what I had learned, and should have stayed longer. Anyhow I wandered away on a glorious botanical and geological excursion, which has lasted nearly fifty years and is not yet completed, always happy and free, poor and rich, without thought of a diploma or of making a name, urged on and on through endless, inspiring, Godful beauty.

From the top of a hill on the north side of Lake Mendota I gained a last wistful, lingering view of the beautiful university grounds and buildings where I had spent so many hungry and happy and hopeful days. There with streaming eyes I bade my blessed alma mater farewell. But I was only leaving one university for another, the Wisconsin University for the University of the Wilderness.

PART TWO:

The Wandering Minstrel

Kentucky Forests and Caves and Through the Cumberland Mountains

Kentucky Forests and Caves

SEPTEMBER 6.

Started at the earliest bird song in hopes of seeing the great Mammoth Cave before evening. Overtook an old Negro driving an ox team. Rode within a few miles and had some interesting chat concerning war, wild fruits of the woods, et cetera. "Right heah," said he, "is where the Rebs was a-tearin' up the track and they all a sudden thought they seed the Yankees a-comin', obah dem big hills dar, and Lo'd, how dey run." I asked him if he would like a renewal of these sad war times, when his flexible face suddenly calmed, and he said with intense earnestness, "Oh, Lo'd, want no mo wa, Lo'd no." Many of these Kentucky Negroes are shrewd and intelligent, and when warmed upon a subject that interests them, are eloquent in no mean degree.

Arrived at Horse Cave. . . . The entrance is by a long easy slope of several hundred yards. It seems like a noble gateway to the birthplace of springs and fountains and the dark treasuries of the mineral kingdom. This cave is in a village (of the same name) which it supplies with an abundance of cold water, and cold air that issues from its fern-clad lips. In hot weather crowds of people sit about it in the shade of the trees that guard it. This magnificent fan is capable of cooling everybody in the town at once. . . . The villager who accompanied me said that Horse Cave had never been fully explored but that it was several miles in length at least. He told me that he had never been at Mammoth Cave—that it was not worth going ten miles to see, as it was nothing but a hole in the ground, and I found that his was no rare case. He was one of the useful, practical men—too wise to waste precious time with weeds, caves, fossils, or anything else that he could not eat.

Arrived at the great Mammoth Cave. I was surprised to find it in so complete naturalness. A large hotel with fine walks and gardens is near it. But fortunately the cave has been un-improved, and were it not for the narrow trail that leads down the glen to its door, one would not know that it had been visited. There are house-rooms and halls whose entrances give but slight hint of their grandeur. And so this magnificent hall in the mineral kingdom of Kentucky has a door comparatively small and unpromising. One might pass within a few yards of it without noticing it.

SEPTEMBER 7.

Left the hospitable Kentuckians with their sincere good wishes and bore away southward again through the deep green woods. In noble forests all day. Saw mistletoe for the first time. Part of the day I traveled with a Kentuckian from near Burkesville. He spoke to all the Negroes he met with familiar kindly greetings, addressing them always as "Uncles" and "Aunts." All travelers one meets on these roads, white and black, male and female, travel on horseback.

SEPTEMBER 8.

Deep, green, bossy sea of waving, flowing hilltops. Corn and cotton and tobacco fields scattered here and there. . . . Met a great many Negroes going to meeting, dressed in their Sunday best. Fat, happy looking, and contented. The scenery on approaching the Cumberland River becomes still grander. Burkesville, in beautiful location, is embosomed in a glorious array of verdant flowing hills. The Cumberland must be a happy stream. I think I could enjoy traveling with it in the midst of such beauty all my life.

Through the Cumberland Mountains

SEPTEMBER 12.

Awoke drenched with mountain mist, which made a grand show, as it moved away before the hot sun. Passed Montgomery, a shabby village at the head of the east slope of the Cumberland Mountains. Obtained breakfast in a clean house and began the descent of the mountains. Obtained fine views of a wide, open country, and distant flanking ridges and spurs. Crossed a wide cool stream [Emory River], a branch of the Clinch River. There is nothing more eloquent in nature than a mountain stream, and this is the first I ever saw. Its banks are luxuriantly peopled with rare and lovely flowers and overarching trees, making one of Nature's coolest and most hospitable places. Every tree, every flower, every ripple and eddy of this lovely stream seemed solemnly to feel the presence of the great Creator. Lingered in this sanctuary a long time, thanking the Lord with all my heart for his goodness in allowing me to enter and enjoy it.

Discovered two ferns, *Dicksonia* and a small matted polypod on trees, common farther south. Also a species of magnolia with very large leaves and scarlet conical fruit. Near this stream I spent some joyous time in a grand rock dwelling full of mosses, birds, and flowers. Most heavenly place I ever entered. The long, narrow valleys of the mountainside, all well watered and nobly adorned with oaks, magnolias, laurels, azaleas, asters, ferns, *Hypnurn* mosses, *Madotheca* [scale mosses], etc. Also towering clumps of beautiful hemlocks. The hemlock, judging from the common species of Canada, I regarded as the least noble of the conifers. But those of the eastern valleys of the Cumberland Mountains are as perfect in form and regal in port as the pines themselves. The latter abundant. Obtained fine glimpses from open places as I descended to the great valley between these mountains and the Unaka Mountains on the state line. Forded the Clinch, a beautiful clear stream that knows many of the dearest mountain retreats that ever heard the music of running water. Reached Kingston before dark. Sent back my plant collections by express to my brother in Wisconsin.

SEPTEMBER 13.

Walked all day across small parallel valleys that flute the surface of the one wide valley. These flutings appear to have been formed by lateral pressure, are fertile, and contain some fine forms, though the seal of war is on all things. The roads never seem to proceed

with any fixed purpose, but wander as if lost. In seeking the way to
Philadelphia [in Loudon County, Tennessee], I was told by a buxom
Tennessee "gal" that over the hills was much the nearer way, that
she always went that way, and that surely I could travel it.

I started over the flint ridges, but soon reached a set of enchanted
little valleys among which, no matter how or in what direction
I traveled, I could not get a foot nearer to Philadelphia. At last,
consulting my map and compass, I neglected all directions and
finally reached the house of a Negro driver, with whom I put up
for the night. Received a good deal of knowledge which may be of
use should I ever be a Negro teamster.

SEPTEMBER 14.
Philadelphia is a very filthy village in a beautiful situation. More
or less of pine. Black oak most abundant. *Polypodium hexagonop-
terum* and *Aspidium acrostichoides* [Christmas fern] most abundant of
ferns and most generally distributed. *Osmunda claytoniana* rare, not
in fruit, small. *Dicksonia* abundant after leaving the Cumberland
Mountains. *Asplenium ebeneum* [ebony spleenwort] quite common
in Tennessee and many parts of Kentucky. *Cystopteris* [bladder fern],
and *Asplenium filix-foemina* not common through the same range.
Pteris aquilina [common brake] abundant, but small.

Walked through many a leafy valley, shady grove, and cool
brooklet. Reached Madisonville, a brisk village. Came in full view
of the Unaka Mountains, a magnificent sight. Stayed overnight
with a pleasant young farmer.

The River Country of Georgia, Through Florida's Swamps and Forests, and across Florida to Cedar Keys

The River Country of Georgia

OCTOBER 3.

In "pine barrens" most of the day. Low, level, sandy tracts; the pines wide apart; the sunny spaces between full of beautiful abounding grasses, *Liatris*, long, wandlike *Solidago*, saw palmettos, etc., covering the ground in garden style. Here I sauntered in delightful freedom, meeting none of the cat-clawed vines, or shrubs, of the alluvial bottoms. Dwarf live oaks common.

Toward evening I arrived at the home of Mr. Cameron, a wealthy planter, who had large bands of slaves at work in his cotton fields. They still call him "Massa." He tells me that labor costs him less now than it did before the emancipation of the Negroes. When I arrived I found him busily engaged in scouring the rust off some cotton-gin saws which had been lying for months at the bottom of his millpond to prevent Sherman's "bummers" from destroying them. The most valuable parts of the gristmill and cotton press were hidden in the same way. "If Bill Sherman," he said, "should come down now without his army, he would never go back."

When I asked him if he could give me food and lodging for the night he said, "No, no, we have no accommodations for travelers." I said, "But I am traveling as a botanist and either have to find lodgings when night overtakes me or lie outdoors, which I often have had to do in my long walk from Indiana. But you see that the country here is very swampy. If you will at least sell me a piece of bread and give me a drink at your well, I shall have to look around for a dry spot to lie down on."

Then, asking me a few questions, and narrowly examining me, he said, "Well, it is barely possible that we may find a place for you, and if you will come to the house I will ask my wife." Evidently he was cautious to get his wife's opinion of the kind of creature I was before committing himself to hospitality. He halted me at the door and called out his wife, a fine-looking woman, who also questioned me narrowly as to my object in coming so far down through the South, so soon after the war. She said to her husband that she thought they could, perhaps, give me a place to sleep.

After supper, as we sat by the fire talking on my favorite subject of botany, I described the country I had passed through, its botanical character, etc. Then, evidently, all doubt as to my being a decent man vanished, and they both said that they wouldn't for anything have turned me away; but I must excuse their caution, for perhaps fewer than one in a hundred, who passed through this unfrequented part of the country were to be relied upon. "Only a short time ago we entertained a man who was well spoken and well dressed, and he vanished some time during the night with some valuable silverware."

Mr. Cameron told me that when I arrived he tried me for a Mason, and finding that I was not a Mason he wondered still more that I would venture into the country without being able to gain the assistance of brother Masons in these troublous times.

"Young man," he said, after hearing my talks on botany, "I see that your hobby is botany. My hobby is e-lec-tricity. I believe that the time is coming, though we may not live to see it, when that mysterious power or force, used now only for telegraphy, will eventually supply the power for running railroad trains and steamships, for lighting and, in a word, electricity will do all the work of the world."

Many times since then I have thought of the wonderfully correct vision of this Georgia planter, so far in advance of almost everybody else in the world. Already nearly all that he foresaw has been accomplished, and the use of electricity is being extended more and more every year.

OCTOBER 4.
New plants constantly appearing. All day in dense, wet, dark, mysterious forest of flat-topped *Taxodiums.*

Through Florida Swamps and Forests

OCTOBER 18.
Am walking on land that is almost dry. The dead levels are interrupted here and there by sandy waves a few feet in height. It is said that not a point in all Florida is more than three hundred feet above sea-level—a country where but little grading is required for roads, but much bridging and boring of many tunnels through forests.

Before reaching this open ground, in a lonely, swampy place in the woods, I met a large, muscular, brawny young Negro, who eyed me with glaring, wistful curiosity. I was very thirsty at the time, and inquired of the man if there were any houses or springs near by where I could get a drink. "Oh, yes," he replied, still eagerly searching me with his wild eyes. Then he inquired where I came from, where I was going, and what brought me to such a wild country, where I was liable to be robbed, and perhaps killed.

"Oh, I am not afraid of any one robbing me," I said, "for I don't carry anything worth stealing." "Yes," said he, "but you can't travel without money." I started to walk on, but he blocked my way. Then I noticed that he was trembling, and it flashed upon me all at once that he was thinking of knocking me down in order to rob me. After glaring at my pockets as if searching for weapons, he stammered in a quavering voice, "Do you carry shooting-irons?" His motives, which I ought to have noted sooner, now were apparent to me. Though I had no pistol, I instinctively threw my hand back to my pistol pocket and, with my eyes fled on his, I marched up close to him and said, "I allow people to find out if I am armed or not." Then he quailed, stepped aside, and allowed me to pass, for fear of being shot. This was evidently a narrow escape.

A few miles farther on I came to a cotton-field, to patches of sugar cane carefully fenced, and some respectable-looking houses with gardens. These little fenced fields look as if they were intended to be for plants what cages are for birds. Discovered a large, treelike cactus in a dooryard; a small species was abundant on the sand-hillocks. Reached Gainesville late in the night.

When within three or four miles of the town I noticed a light off in the pine woods. As I was very thirsty, I thought I would venture toward it with the hope of obtaining water. In creeping cautiously and noiselessly through the grass to discover whether or no it was a camp of robber Negroes, I came suddenly in full view of the best-lighted and most primitive of all the domestic establishments I have yet seen in town or grove. There was, first of all, a big, glowing log fire, illuminating the overleaning bushes and trees, bringing out leaf and spray with more than noonday distinctness, and making still darker the surrounding wood. In the center of this globe of light sat two Negroes. I could see their ivory gleaming from the great lips, and their smooth cheeks flashing off light as if made of glass. Seen anywhere but in the South, the glossy pair would have been taken for twin devils, but here it was only a Negro and his wife at their supper.

I ventured forward to the radiant presence of the black pair, and, after being stared at with that desperate fixedness which is said to subdue the lion, I was handed water in a gourd from somewhere out of the darkness. I was standing for a moment beside the big fire, looking at the unsurpassable simplicity of the establishment, and asking questions about the road to Gainesville, when my attention was called to a black lump of something lying in the ashes of the fire. It seemed to be made of rubber; but ere I had time for much speculation, the woman bent wooingly over the black object and said with motherly kindness, "Come, honey, eat yo' hominy."

At the sound of "hominy" the rubber gave strong manifestations of vitality and proved to be a burly little Negro boy, rising from the earth naked as to the earth he came. Had he emerged from the black muck of a marsh, we might easily have believed that the Lord had manufactured him like Adam direct from the earth.

Surely, thought I, as I started for Gainesville, surely I am now coming to the tropics, where the inhabitants wear nothing but their own skins. This fashion is sufficiently simple, "no trouble-some disguises," as Milton calls clothing,—but it certainly is not quite in harmony with Nature. Birds make nests and nearly all beasts make some kind of bed for their young; but these Negroes allow their younglings to lie nestless and naked in the dirt.

Gainesville is rather attractive—an oasis in the desert, compared with other villages. It gets its life from the few plantations located about it on dry ground that rises islandlike a few feet above the swamps. Obtained food and lodging at a sort of tavern.

OCTOBER 22.

This morning I was easily prevailed upon by the captain and an ex-judge, who was rusticating here, to join in a deer hunt. Had a delightful ramble in the long grass and flowery barrens. Started one deer but did not draw a single shot. The captain, the judge, and myself stood at different stations where the deer was expected to pass, while a brother of the captain entered the woods to arouse the game from cover. The one deer that he started took a direction different from any which this particular old buck had ever been known to take in times past, and in so doing was cordially cursed as being the "d-----dest deer that ever ran unshot." To me it appeared as "d-----dest" work to slaughter God's cattle for sport. "They were made for us," say these self-approving preachers; "for our food, our recreation, or other uses not yet discovered." As truthfully we might say on behalf of a bear, when he deals successfully with an unfortunate hunter, "Men and other bipeds were made for bears, and thanks be to God for claws and teeth so long."

Let a Christian hunter go to the Lord's woods and kill his well-kept beasts, or wild Indians, and it is well; but let an enterprising specimen of these proper, predestined victims go to houses and fields and kill the most worthless person of the vertical godlike killers,—oh! that is horribly unorthodox, and on the part of the Indians atrocious murder! Well, I have precious little sympathy for the selfish propriety of civilized man, and if a war of races should occur between the wild beasts and Lord Man, I would be tempted to sympathize with the bears.

Cedar Keys

OCTOBER 23.

Today I reached the sea. While I was yet many miles back in the palmy woods, I caught the scent of the salt sea breeze which, although I had so many years lived far from sea breezes, suddenly conjured up Dunbar, its rocky coast, winds and waves; and my whole childhood, which seemed to have utterly vanished in the New World, was now restored amid the Florida woods by that one breath from the sea. Forgotten were the palms and magnolias and the thousand flowers that enclosed me. I could see only dulse and tangle, long-winged gulls, the Bass Rock in the Firth of Forth, and the old castle, schools, churches, and long country rambles in search of birds' nests. I do not wonder that the weary camels coming from the scorching African deserts should be able to scent the Nile.

How imperishable are all the impressions that ever vibrate one's life! We cannot forget anything. Memories may escape the action of will, may sleep a long time, but when stirred by the right influence, though that influence be light as a shadow, they flash into full stature and life with everything in place. For nineteen years my vision was bounded by forests, but today, emerging from a multitude of tropical plants, I beheld the Gulf of Mexico stretching away unbounded, except by the sky. What dreams and speculative matter for thought arose as I stood on the strand, gazing out on the burnished, treeless plain!

But now at the seaside I was in difficulty. I had reached a point that I could not ford, and Cedar Keys had an empty harbor. Would I proceed down the peninsula to Tampa and Key West, where I would be sure to find a vessel for Cuba, or would I wait here, like Crusoe, and pray for a ship. Full of these thoughts, I stepped into a little store which had a considerable trade in quinine and alligator and rattlesnake skins, and inquired about shipping, means of travel, etc.

The proprietor informed me that one of several sawmills near the village was running, and that a schooner chartered to carry a load of lumber to Galveston, Texas, was expected at the mills for a load. This mill was situated on a tongue of land a few miles along the coast from Cedar Keys, and I determined to see Mr. Hodgson, the owner, to find out particulars about the expected schooner, the time she would take to load, whether I would be likely to obtain passage on her, etc.

Found Mr. Hodgson at his mill. Stated my case, and was kindly furnished the desired information. I determined to wait the two weeks likely to elapse before she sailed, and go on her to the flowery plains of Texas, from any of whose ports, I fancied, I could easily find passage to the West Indies. I agreed to work for Mr. Hodgson in the mill until I sailed, as I had but little money. He invited me to his spacious house, which occupied a shell hillock and commanded a fine view of the Gulf and many gems of palmy islets, called "keys," that fringe the shore like huge bouquets—not too big, however, for the spacious waters. Mr. Hodgson's family welcomed me with that open, unconstrained cordiality which is characteristic of the better class of Southern people.

At the sawmill a new cover had been put on the main driving pulley, which, made of rough plank, had to be turned off and smoothed. He asked me if I was able to do this job, and I told him that I could. Fixing a rest and making a tool out of an old file, I directed the engineer to start the engine and run slow. After turning down the pulley and getting it true, I put a keen edge on a common carpenter's plane, quickly finished the job, and was assigned a bunk in one of the employees' lodging houses.

The next day I felt a strange dullness and headache while I was botanizing along the coast. Thinking that a bath in the salt water might refresh me, I plunged in and swam a little distance, but this seemed only to make me feel worse. I felt anxious for something sour, and walked back to the village to buy lemons.

Thus and here my long walk was interrupted. I thought that a few days' sail would land me among the famous flower beds of Texas. But the expected ship came and went while I was helpless with fever. The very day after reaching the sea I began to be weighed down by inexorable leaden numbness, which I resisted and tried to shake off for three days, by bathing in the Gulf, by dragging myself about among the palms, plants, and strange shells of the shore, and by doing a little mill work. I did not fear any serious illness, for I never was sick before and was unwilling to pay attention to my feelings.

But yet heavier and more remorselessly pressed the growing fever, rapidly gaining on my strength. On the third day after my arrival I could not take any nourishment, but craved acid. Cedar Keys was only a mile or two distant, and I managed to walk there to buy lemons. On returning, about the middle of the afternoon, the fever broke on me like a storm, and before I had staggered halfway to the mill I fell down unconscious on the narrow trail among dwarf palmettos.

When I awoke from the hot fever sleep, the stars were shining and I was at a loss to know which end of the trail to take, but fortunately, as it afterwards proved, I guessed right. Subsequently, as I fell again and again after walking only a hundred yards or so, I was careful to lie with my head in the direction in which I thought the mill was. I rose, staggered, and fell, I know not how many times, in delirious bewilderment, gasping and throbbing with only moments of consciousness. Thus passed the hours till after midnight, when I reached the mill lodging house.

The watchman on his rounds found me lying on a heap of sawdust at the foot of the stairs. I asked him to assist me up the steps to bed, but he thought my difficulty was only intoxication and refused to help me. The mill hands, especially on Saturday nights, often returned from the village drunk. This was the cause of the watchman's refusal. Feeling that I must get to bed, I made out to reach it on hands and knees, tumbled in after a desperate struggle, and immediately became oblivious to everything.

I awoke at a strange hour on a strange day to hear Mr. Hodgson ask a watcher beside me whether I had yet spoken, and when he replied that I had not, he said: "Well, you must keep on pouring in quinine. That's all we can do." How long I lay unconscious I never found out, but it must have been many days. Some time or other I was moved on a horse from the mill quarters to Mr. Hodgson's house, where I was nursed about three months with unfailing kindness, and to the skill and care of Mr. and Mrs. Hodgson I doubtless owe my life. Through quinine and calomel—in sorry abundance—with other milder medicines, my malarial fever became typhoid. I had night sweats, and my legs became like posts of the temper and consistency of clay on account of dropsy. So on until January, a weary time.

As soon as I was able to get out of bed, I crept away to the edge of the wood and sat, day after day, beneath a moss-draped live oak, watching birds feeding on the shore when the tide was out. Later, as I gathered some strength, I sailed in a little skiff from one key to another. Nearly all the shrubs and trees here are evergreen, and a few of the smaller plants are in flower all winter. The principal trees on this Cedar Key are the juniper, long-leafed pine, and live oak. All of the latter, living and dead, are heavily draped with *Tillandsia*, like those of Bonaventure. The leaf is oval, about two inches long, three-fourths of an inch wide, glossy and dark green above, pale beneath. The trunk is usually much-divided, and is extremely unwedgeable. The specimen on the opposite page [of the original journal] is growing in the dooryard of Mr. Hodgson's house. It is a grand old king, whose crown gleamed in the bright sky long ere the Spanish shipbuilders felled a single tree of this noble species.

The live oaks of these keys divide empire with the long-leafed pine and palmetto, but in many places on the mainland there are large tracts exclusively occupied by them. Like the Bonaventure oaks, they have the upper side of their main spreading branches thickly planted with ferns, grasses, small saw palmettos, etc. There is also a dwarf oak here, which forms dense thickets. The oaks of this key are not, like those of the Wisconsin openings, growing on grassy slopes, but stand, sunk to the shoulders, in flowering magnolias, heathworts, etc.

During my long sojourn here as a convalescent I used to lie on my back for whole days beneath the ample arms of these great trees, listening to the winds and the birds. There is an extensive shallow on the coast, close by, which the receding tide exposes daily. This is the feeding-ground of thousands of waders of all sizes, plumage, and language, and they make a lively picture and noise when they gather at the great family board to eat their daily bread, so bountifully provided for them.

Their leisure in time of high tide they spend in various ways and places. Some go in large flocks to reedy margins about the islands and wade and stand about quarreling or making sport, occasionally finding a stray mouthful to eat. Some stand on the mangroves of the solitary shore, now and then plunging into the water after a fish. Some go long journeys inland, up creeks and inlets. A few lonely old herons of solemn look and wing retire to favorite oaks. It was my delight to watch those old white sages of immaculate feather as they stood erect drowsing away the dull hours between tides, curtained by long skeins of *Tillandsia*. White-bearded hermits gazing dreamily from dark caves could not appear more solemn or more becomingly shrouded from the rest of their fellow beings.

One of the characteristic plants of these keys is the Spanish bayonet, a species of *Yucca*, about eight or ten feet in height, and with a trunk three or four inches in diameter when full-grown. It belongs to the lily family and develops palm-like from terminal buds. The stout leaves are very rigid, sharp-pointed, and bayonet-like. By one of these leaves a man might be as seriously stabbed as by an army bayonet, and woe to the luckless wanderer who dares to urge his way through these armed gardens after dark. Vegetable cats of many species will rob him of his clothes and claw his flesh, while dwarf palmettos will saw his bones, and the bayonets will glide to his joints and marrow without the smallest consideration for Lord Man.

The climate of these precious islets is simply warm summer and warmer summer, corresponding in time with winter and summer in the North. The weather goes smoothly over the points of union betwixt the twin summers. Few of the storms are very loud or variable. The average temperature during the day, in December, was about sixty-five degrees in the shade, but on one day a little damp snow fell.

Cedar Key is two-and-one-half or three miles in diameter, and its highest point is forty-four feet above mean tidewater. It is surrounded by scores of other keys, many of them looking like a clump of palms, arranged like a tasteful bouquet, and placed in the sea to be kept fresh. Others have quite a sprinkling of oaks and junipers, beautifully united with vines. Still others consist of shells, with a few grasses and mangroves, circled with a rim of rushes. Those which have sedgy margins furnish a favorite retreat for countless waders and divers, especially for the pelicans that frequently whiten the shore like a ring of foam.

It is delightful to observe the assembling of these feathered people from the woods and reedy isles; herons white as wave-tops, or blue as the sky, winnowing the warm air on wide, quiet wing; pelicans coming with baskets to fill, and the multitude of smaller sailors of the air, swift as swallows, gracefully taking their places at Nature's family table for their daily bread. Happy birds!

PART THREE:

The Nature Scribe and Rhapsode

In Camp on the North Fork of the Merced

JUNE 16.

One of the Indians from Brown's Flat got right into the middle of the camp this morning, unobserved. I was seated on a stone, looking over my notes and sketches, and happening to look up, was startled to see him standing grim and silent within a few steps of me, as motionless and weather-stained as an old tree-stump that had stood there for centuries. All Indians seem to have learned this wonderful way of walking unseen,—making themselves invisible like certain spiders I have been observing here, which, in case of alarm, caused, for example, by a bird alighting on the bush their webs are spread upon, immediately bounce themselves up and down on their elastic threads so rapidly that only a blur is visible. The wild Indian power of escaping observation, even where there is little or no cover to hide in, was probably slowly acquired in hard hunting and fighting lessons while trying to approach game, take enemies by surprise, or get safely away when compelled to retreat. And this experience transmitted through many generations seems at length to have become what is vaguely called instinct.

How smooth and changeless seems the surface of the mountains about us! Scarce a track is to be found beyond the range of the sheep except on small open spots on the sides of the streams, or where the forest carpets are thin or wanting. On the smoothest of these open strips and patches deer tracks may be seen, and the great suggestive footprints of bears, which, with those of the many small animals, are scarce enough to answer as a kind of light ornamental stitching or embroidery. Along the main ridges and larger branches of the river Indian trails may be traced, but they are not nearly as distinct as one would expect to find them. How many centuries Indians have roamed these woods nobody knows, probably a great many, extending far beyond the time that Columbus touched our shores, and it seems strange that heavier marks have not been made. Indians walk softly and hurt the landscape hardly more than the birds and squirrels, and their brush and bark huts last hardly longer than those of wood rats, while their more enduring monuments, excepting those wrought on the forests by the fires they made to improve their hunting grounds, vanish in a few centuries.

How different are most of those of the white man, especially on the lower gold region,—roads blasted in the solid rock, wild streams dammed and tamed and turned out of their channels and led along the sides of cañons and valleys to work in mines like slaves. Crossing from ridge to ridge, high in the air, on long straddling trestles as if flowing on stilts, or down and up across valleys and hills, imprisoned in iron pipes to strike and wash away hills and miles of the skin of the mountain's face, riddling, stripping every gold gully and flat. These are the white man's marks made in a few feverish years, to say nothing of mills, fields, villages, scattered hundreds of miles along the flank of the Range. Long will it be ere these marks are effaced, though Nature is doing what she can, replanting, gardening, sweeping away old dams and flumes, leveling gravel and boulder piles, patiently trying to heal every raw scar. The main gold storm is over. Calm enough are the gray old miners scratching a bare living in waste diggings here and there. Thundering underground blasting is still going on to feed the pounding quartz mills, but their influence on the landscape is light as compared with that of the pick-and-shovel storms waged a few years ago. Fortunately for Sierra scenery the gold-bearing slates are mostly restricted to the foothills. The region about our camp is still wild, and higher lies the snow about as trackless as the sky.

Only a few hills and domes of cloudland were built yesterday and none at all to-day. The light is peculiarly white and thin, though pleasantly warm. The serenity of this mountain weather in the spring, just when Nature's pulses are beating highest, is one of its greatest charms. There is only a moderate breeze from the summits of the Range at night, and a slight breathing from the sea and the lowland hills and plains during the day, or stillness so complete no leaf stirs. The trees hereabouts have but little wind history to tell.

Sheep, like people, are ungovernable when hungry. Excepting my guarded lily gardens, almost every leaf that these hoofed locusts can reach within a radius of a mile or two from camp has been devoured. Even the bushes are stripped bare, and in spite of dogs and shepherds the sheep scatter to all points of the compass and vanish in dust. I fear some are lost, for one of the sixteen black ones is missing.

JUNE 17.

Counted the wool bundles this morning as they bounced through the narrow corral gate. About three hundred are missing, and as the shepherd could not go to seek them, I had to go. I tied a crust of bread to my belt, and with Carlo set out for the upper slopes of the Pilot Peak Ridge, and had a good day, notwithstanding the care of seeking the silly runaways. I went out for wool, and did not come back shorn. A peculiar light circled around the horizon, white and thin like that often seen over the auroral corona, blending into the blue of the upper sky. The only clouds were a few faint flossy pencilings like combed silk. I pushed direct to the boundary of the usual range of the flock, and around it until I found the outgoing trail of the wanderers. It led far up the ridge into an open place surrounded by a hedge-like growth of ceanothus chaparral. Carlo knew what I was about, and eagerly followed the scent until we came up to them, huddled in a timid, silent bunch. They had evidently been here all night and all the forenoon, afraid to go out to feed. Having escaped restraint, they were, like some people we know of, afraid of their freedom, did not know what to do with it, and seemed glad to get back into the old familiar bondage.

JUNE 18.

Another inspiring morning, nothing better in any world can be conceived. No description of Heaven that I have ever heard or read of seems half so fine. At noon the clouds occupied about .05 of the sky, white filmy touches drawn delicately on the azure.

The high ridges and hilltops beyond the woolly locusts are now gay with monardella, clarkia, coreopsis, and tall tufted grasses, some of them tall enough to wave like pines. The lupines, of which there are many ill-defined species, are now mostly out of flower, and many of the composite are beginning to fade, their radiant corollas vanishing in fluffy pappus like stars in mist.

We had another visitor from Brown's Flat to-day, an old Indian woman with a basket on her back. Like our first caller from the village, she got fairly into camp and was standing in plain view when discovered. How long she had been quietly looking on, I cannot say. Even the dogs failed to notice her stealthy approach. She was on her way, I suppose, to some wild garden, probably for lupine and starchy saxifrage leaves and rootstocks. Her dress was calico rags, far from clean. In every way she seemed sadly unlike Nature's neat well-dressed animals, though living like them on the bounty of the wilderness. Strange that mankind alone is dirty. Had she been clad in fur, or cloth woven of grass or shreddy bark, like the juniper and libocedrus mats, she might then have seemed a rightful part of the wilderness; like a good wolf at least, or bear. But from no point of view that I have found are such debased fellow beings a whit more natural than the glaring tailored tourists we saw that frightened the birds and squirrels.

The Mono Indians of Bloody Cañon

AUGUST 21.

Have just returned from a fine wild excursion across the range to Mono Lake, by way of the Mono or Bloody Cañon Pass. Mr. Delaney has been good to me all summer, lending a helping, sympathizing hand at every opportunity, as if my wild notions and rambles and studies were his own. He is one of those remarkable California men who have been overflowed and denuded and remodeled by the excitements of the gold fields, like the Sierra landscapes by grinding ice, bringing the harder bosses and ridges of character into relief,—a tall, lean, big-boned, big-hearted Irishman, educated for a priest in Maynooth College,—lots of good in him, shining out now and then in this mountain light. Recognizing my love of wild places, he told me one evening that I ought to go through Bloody Cañon, for he was sure I should find it wild enough. He had not been there himself, he said, but had heard many of his mining friends speak of it as the wildest of all the Sierra passes. Of course I was glad to go. It lies just to the east of our camp and swoops down from the summit of the range to the edge of the Mono Desert, making a descent of about four thousand feet in a distance of about four miles. It was known and traveled as a pass by wild animals and the Indians long before its discovery by white men in the gold year of 1858, as is shown by old trails which come together at the head of it. The name may have been suggested by the red color of the metamorphic slates in which the cañon abounds, or by the blood stains on the rocks from the unfortunate animals that were compelled to slide and shuffle over the sharp-angled boulders.

Early in the morning I tied my notebook and some bread to my belt, and strode away full of eager hope, feeling that I was going to have a glorious revel. The glacier meadows that lay along my way served to soothe my morning speed, for the sod was full of blue gentians and daisies, kalmia and dwarf vaccinium, calling for recognition as old friends, and I had to stop many times to examine the shining rocks over which the ancient glacier had passed with tremendous pressure, polishing them so well that they reflected the sunlight like glass in some places, while fine striæ, seen clearly through a lens, indicated the direction in which the ice had flowed. On some of the sloping polished pavements abrupt steps occur, showing that occasionally large masses of the rock had given way before the glacial pressure, as well as small particles; moraines, too, some scattered, others regular like long curving embankments and dams, occur here and there, giving the general surface of the region a young, new-made appearance. I watched the gradual dwarfing of the pines as I ascended, and the corresponding dwarfing of nearly all the rest of the vegetation. On the slopes of Mammoth Mountain, to the south of the pass, I saw many gaps in the woods reaching from the upper edge of the timber-line down to the level meadows, where avalanches of snow had descended, sweeping away every tree in their paths as well as the soil they were growing in, leaving the bedrock bare. The trees are nearly all uprooted, but a few that had been extremely well anchored in clefts of the rock were broken off near the ground. It seems strange at first sight that trees that had been allowed to grow for a century or more undisturbed should in their old age be thus swished away at a stroke. Such avalanches can only occur under rare conditions of weather and snowfall. No doubt on some positions of the mountain slopes the inclination and smoothness of the surface is such that avalanches must occur every winter, or even after every heavy snowstorm, and of course no trees or even bushes can grow in their channels. I noticed a few clean-swept slopes of this kind. The uprooted trees that had grown in the pathway of what might be called "century avalanches" were piled in windrows, and tucked snugly against the wall-trees of the gaps, heads downward, excepting a few that were carried out into the open ground of the meadows, where the heads of the avalanches had stopped. Young pines, mostly the two-leaved and the white-barked, are already springing up in these cleared gaps. It would be interesting to ascertain the age of these saplings, for thus we should gain a fair approximation to the year that the great avalanches occurred. Perhaps most or all of them occurred the same winter. How glad I should be if free to pursue such studies!

Near the summit at the head of the pass I found a species of dwarf willow lying perfectly flat on the ground, making a nice, soft, silky gray carpet, not a single stem or branch more than three inches high; but the catkins, which are now nearly ripe, stand erect and make a close, nearly regular gray growth, being larger than all the rest of the plants. Some of these interesting dwarfs have only one catkin—willow bushes reduced to their lowest terms. I found patches of dwarf vaccinium also forming smooth carpets, closely pressed to the ground or against the sides of stones, and covered with round pink flowers in lavish abundance as if they had fallen from the sky like hail. A little higher, almost at the very head of the pass, I found the blue arctic daisy and purple-flowered bryanthus, the mountain's own darlings, gentle mountaineers face to face with the sky, kept safe and warm by a thousand miracles, seeming always the finer and purer the wilder and stormier their homes. The trees, tough and resiny, seem unable to go a step farther; but up and up, far above the tree-line, these tender plants climb, cheerily spreading their gray and pink carpets right up to the very edges of the snow-banks in deep hollows and shadows. Here, too, is the familiar robin, tripping on the flowery lawns, bravely singing the same cheery song I first heard when a boy in Wisconsin newly arrived from old Scotland. In this fine company sauntering enchanted, taking no heed of time, I at length entered the gate of the pass, and the huge rocks began to close around me in all their mysterious impressiveness. Just then I was startled by a lot of queer, hairy, muffled creatures coming shuffling, shambling, wallowing toward me as if they had no bones in their bodies. Had I discovered them while they were yet a good way off, I should have tried to avoid them. What a picture they made contrasted with the others I had just been admiring. When I came up to them, I found that they were only a band of Indians from Mono on their way to Yosemite for a load of acorns. They were wrapped in blankets made of the skins of sage-rabbits. The dirt on some of the faces seemed almost old enough and thick enough to have a geological significance; some were strangely blurred and divided into sections by seams and wrinkles that looked like cleavage joints, and had a worn abraded look as if they had lain exposed to the weather for ages. I tried to pass them without stopping, but they wouldn't let me; forming a dismal circle about me, I was closely besieged while they begged whiskey or tobacco, and it was hard to convince them that I hadn't any. How glad I was to get away from the gray, grim crowd and see them vanish down the trail! Yet it seems sad to feel such desperate repulsion from one's fellow beings, however degraded. To prefer the society of squirrels and woodchucks to that of our own species must surely be unnatural. So with a fresh breeze and a hill or mountain between us I must wish them Godspeed and try to pray and sing with Burns, "It's coming yet, for a' that, that man to man, the warld o'er, shall brothers be for a' that."

How the day passed I hardly know. By the map I have come only about ten or twelve miles, though the sun is already low in the west, showing how long I must have lingered, observing, sketching, taking notes among the glaciated rocks and moraines and Alpine flower-beds.

At sundown the somber crags and peaks were inspired with the ineffable beauty of the alpenglow, and a solemn, awful stillness hushed everything in the landscape. Then I crept into a hollow by the side of a small lake near the head of the cañon, smoothed a sheltered spot, and gathered a few pine tassels for a bed. After the short twilight began to fade I kindled a sunny fire, made a tin cupful of tea, and lay down to watch the stars. Soon the night-wind began to flow from the snowy peaks overhead, at first only a gentle breathing, then gaining strength, in less than an hour rumbled in massive volume something like a boisterous stream in a boulder-choked channel, roaring and moaning down the cañon as if the work it had to do was tremendously important and fateful; and mingled with these storm tones were those of the waterfalls on the north side of the cañon, now sounding distinctly, now smothered by the heavier cataracts of air, making a glorious psalm of savage wildness. My fire squirmed and struggled as if ill at ease, for though in a sheltered nook, detached masses of icy wind often fell like icebergs on top of it, scattering sparks and coals, so that I had to keep well back to avoid being burned. But the big resiny roots and knots of the dwarf pine could neither be beaten out nor blown away, and the flames, now rushing up in long lances, now flattened and twisted on the rocky ground, roared as if trying to tell the storm stories of the trees they belonged to, as the light given out was telling the story of the sunshine they had gathered in centuries of summers.

The stars shone clear in the strip of sky between the huge dark cliffs; and as I lay recalling the lessons of the day, suddenly the full moon looked down over the cañon wall, her face apparently filled with eager concern, which had a startling effect, as if she had left her place in the sky and had come down to gaze on me alone, like a person entering one's bedroom. It was hard to realize that she was in her place in the sky, and was looking abroad on half the globe, land and sea, mountains, plains, lakes, rivers, oceans, ships, cities with their myriads of inhabitants sleeping and waking, sick and well. No, she seemed to be just on the rim of Bloody Cañon and looking only at me. This was indeed getting near to Nature. I remember watching the harvest moon rising above the oak trees in Wisconsin apparently as big as a cart-wheel and not farther than half a mile distant. With these exceptions I might say I never before had seen the moon, and this night she seemed so full of life and so near, the effect was marvelously impressive and made me forget the Indians, the great black rocks above me, and the wild uproar of the winds and waters making their way down the huge jagged gorge. Of course I slept but little and gladly welcomed the dawn over the Mono Desert. By the time I had made a cupful of tea the sunbeams were pouring through the cañon, and I set forth, gazing eagerly at the tremendous walls of red slates savagely hacked and scarred and apparently ready to fall in avalanches great enough to choke the pass and fill up the chain of lakelets. But soon its beauties came to view, and I bounded lightly from rock to rock, admiring the polished bosses shining in the slant sunshine with glorious effect in the general roughness of moraines and avalanche taluses, even toward the head of the cañon near the highest fountains of the ice. Here, too, are most of the lowly plant people seen yesterday on the other side of the divide now opening their beautiful eyes. None could fail to glory in Nature's tender care for them in so wild a place. The little ouzel is flitting from rock to rock along the rapid swirling Cañon Creek, diving for breakfast in icy pools, and merrily singing as if the huge rugged avalanche-swept gorge was the most delightful of all its mountain homes. Besides a high fall on the north wall of the cañon, apparently coming direct from the sky, there are many narrow cascades, bright silvery ribbons zigzagging down the red cliffs, tracing the diagonal cleavage joints of the metamorphic slates, now contracted and out of sight, now leaping from ledge to ledge in filmy sheets through which the sunbeams sift. And on the main Cañon Creek, to which all these are tributary, is a series of small falls, cascades, and rapids extending all the way down to the foot of the cañon, interrupted only by the lakes in which the tossed and beaten waters rest. One of the finest of the cascades is outspread on the face of a precipice, its waters separated into ribbon-like strips, and woven into a diamond-like pattern by tracing the cleavage joints of the rock, while tufts of bryanthus, grass, sedge, saxifrage form beautiful fringes. Who could imagine beauty so fine in so savage a place? Gardens are blooming in all sorts of nooks and hollows,—at the head alpine eriogonums, erigerons, saxifrages, gentians, cowania, bush primula; in the middle region larkspur, columbine, orthocarpus, castilleia, harebell, epilobium, violets, mints, yarrow; near the foot sunflowers, lilies, brier rose, iris, lonicera, clematis.

One of the smallest of the cascades, which I name the Bower Cascade, is in the lower region of the pass, where the vegetation is snowy and luxuriant. Wild rose and dogwood form dense masses overarching the stream, and out of this bower the creek, grown strong with many in dashing tributaries, leaps forth into the light, and descends in a fluted curve thick-sown with crisp flashing spray. At the foot of the cañon there is a lake formed in part at least by the damming of the stream by a terminal moraine. The three other lakes in the cañon are in basins eroded from the solid rock, where the pressure of the glacier was greatest, and the most resisting portions of the basin rims are beautifully, tellingly polished. Below Moraine Lake at the foot of the cañon there are several old lake-basins lying between the large lateral moraines which extend out into the desert. These basins are now completely filled up by the material carried in by the streams, and changed to dry sandy flats covered mostly by grass and artemisia and sun-loving flowers. All these lower lake-basins were evidently formed by terminal moraine dams deposited where the receding glacier had lingered during short periods of less waste, or greater snowfall, or both.

Looking up the cañon from the warm sunny edge of the Mono plain my morning ramble seems a dream, so great is the change in the vegetation and climate. The lilies on the bank of Moraine Lake are higher than my head, and the sunshine is hot enough for palms. Yet the snow round the arctic gardens at the summit of the pass is plainly visible, only about four miles away, and between lie specimen zones of all the principal climates of the globe. In little more than an hour one may swoop down from winter to summer, from an Arctic to a torrid region, through as great changes of climate as one would encounter in traveling from Labrador to Florida.

The Indians I had met near the head of the cañon had camped at the foot of it the night before they made the ascent, and I found their fire still smoking on the side of a small tributary stream near Moraine Lake; and on the edge of what is called the Mono Desert, four or five miles from the lake, I came to a patch of elymus, or wild rye, growing in magnificent waving clumps six or eight feet high, bearing heads six to eight inches long. The crop was ripe, and Indian women were gathering the grain in baskets by bending down large handfuls, beating out the seed, and fanning it in the wind. The grains are about five eighths of an inch long, dark-colored and sweet. I fancy the bread made from it must be as good as wheat bread. A fine squirrelish employment this wild grain gathering seems, and the women were evidently enjoying it, laughing and chattering and looking almost natural, though most Indians I have seen are not a whit more natural in their lives than we civilized whites. Perhaps if I knew them better I should like them better. The worst thing about them is their uncleanliness. Nothing truly wild is unclean. Down on the shore of Mono Lake I saw a number of their flimsy huts on the banks of streams that dash swiftly into that dead sea,—mere brush tents where they lie and eat at their ease. Some of the men were feasting on buffalo berries, lying beneath the tall bushes now red with fruit. The berries are rather insipid, but they must needs be wholesome, since for days and weeks the Indians, it is said, eat nothing else. In the season they in like manner depend chiefly on the fat larvæ of a fly that breeds in the salt water of the lake, or on the big fat corrugated caterpillars of a species of silkworm that feeds on the leaves of the yellow pine. Occasionally a grand rabbit-drive is organized and hundreds are slain with clubs on the lake shore, chased and frightened into a dense crowd by dogs, boys, girls, men and women, and rings of sage brush fire, when of course they are quickly killed. The skins are made into blankets. In the autumn the more enterprising of the hunters bring in a good many deer, and rarely a wild sheep from the high peaks. Antelopes used to be abundant on the desert at the base of the interior mountain-ranges. Sage hens, grouse, and squirrels help to vary their wild diet of worms; pine nuts also from the small interesting *Pinus monophylla*, and good bread and good mush are made from acorns and wild rye. Strange to say, they seem to like the lake larvæ best of all. Long windrows are washed up on the shore, which they gather and dry like grain for winter use. It is said that wars, on account of encroachments on each other's worm-grounds, are of common occurrence among the various tribes and families. Each claims a certain marked portion of the shore. The pine nuts are delicious—large quantities are gathered every autumn. The tribes of the west flank of the range trade acorns for worms and pine nuts. The squaws carry immense loads on their backs across the rough passes and down the range, making journeys of about forty or fifty miles each way.

The desert around the lake is surprisingly flowery. In many places among the sage bushes I saw mentzelia, abronia, aster, bigelovia, and gilia, all of which seemed to enjoy the hot sunshine. The abronia, in particular, is a delicate, fragrant, and most charming plant.

Opposite the mouth of the cañon a range of volcanic cones extends southward from the lake, rising abruptly out of the desert like a chain of mountains. The largest of the cones are about twenty-five hundred feet high above the lake level, have well-formed craters, and all of them are evidently comparatively recent additions to the landscape. At a distance of a few miles they look like heaps of loose ashes that have never been blest by either rain or snow, but, for a' that and a' that, yellow pines are climbing their gray slopes, trying to clothe them and give beauty for ashes. A country of wonderful contrasts. Hot deserts bounded by snow-laden mountains,—cinders and ashes scattered on glacier-polished pavements,—frost and fire working together in the making of beauty. In the lake are several volcanic islands, which show that the waters were once mingled with fire.

Glad to get back to the green side of the mountains, though I have greatly enjoyed the gray east side and hope to see more of it. Reading these grand mountain manuscripts displayed through every vicissitude of heat and cold, calm and storm, upheaving volcanoes and down-grinding glaciers, we see that everything in Nature called destruction must be creation—a change from beauty to beauty.

Our glacier meadow camp north of the Soda Springs seems more beautiful every day. The grass covers all the ground though the leaves are thread-like in fineness, and in walking on the sod it seems like a plush carpet of marvelous richness and softness, and the purple panicles brushing against one's feet are not felt. This is a typical glacier meadow, occupying the basin of a vanished lake, very definitely bounded by walls of the arrowy two-leaved pines drawn up in a handsome orderly array like soldiers on parade.

There are many other meadows of the same kind hereabouts imbedded in the woods. The main big meadows along the river are the same in general and extend with but little interruption for ten or twelve miles, but none I have seen are so finely finished and perfect as this one. It is richer in flowering plants than the prairies of Wisconsin and Illinois were when in all their wild glory. The showy flowers are mostly three species of gentian, a purple and yellow orthocarpus, a golden-rod or two, a small blue pentstemon almost like a gentian, potentilla, ivesia, pedicularis, white violet, kalmia, and bryanthus. There are no coarse weedy plants. Through this flowery lawn flows a stream silently gliding, swirling, slipping as if careful not to make the slightest noise. It is only about three feet wide in most places, widening here and there into pools six or eight feet in diameter with no apparent current, the banks bossily rounded by the down-curving mossy sod, grass panicles overleaning like miniature pine trees, and rugs of bryanthus spreading here and there over sunken boulders. At the foot of the meadow the stream, rich with the juices of the plants it has refreshed, sings merrily down over shelving rock ledges on its way to the Tuolumne River. The sublime, massive Mount Dana and its companions, green, red, and white, loom impressively above the pines along the eastern horizon; a range or spur of gray rugged granite crags and mountains on the north; the curiously crested and battlemented Mount Hoffman on the west; and the Cathedral Range on the south with its grand Cathedral Peak, Cathedral Spires, Unicorn Peak, and several others, gray and pointed or massively rounded.

A Near View of the High Sierra

Early one bright morning in the middle of Indian summer, while the glacier meadows were still crisp with frost crystals, I set out from the foot of Mount Lyell on my way down to Yosemite Valley, to replenish my exhausted store of bread and tea. I had spent the past summer, as many preceding ones, exploring the glaciers that lie on the head waters of the San Joaquin, Tuolumne, Merced, and Owen's rivers; measuring and studying their movements, trends, crevasses, moraines, etc., and the part they had played during the period of their greater extension in the creation and development of the landscapes of this alpine wonderland. The time for this kind of work was nearly over for the year, and I began to look forward with delight to the approaching winter with its wondrous storms, when I would be warmly snowbound in my Yosemite cabin with plenty of bread and books; but a tinge of regret came on when I considered that possibly I might not see this favorite region again until the next summer, excepting distant views from the heights about the Yosemite walls.

To artists, few portions of the High Sierra are, strictly speaking, picturesque. The whole massive uplift of the range is one great picture, not clearly divisible into smaller ones; differing much in this respect from the older, and what may be called, riper mountains of the Coast Range. All the landscapes of the Sierra, as we have seen, were born again, remodeled from base to summit by the developing ice floods of the last glacial winter. But all these new landscapes were not brought forth simultaneously; some of the highest, where the ice lingered longest, are tens of centuries younger than those of the warmer regions below them. In general, the younger the mountain landscapes—younger, I mean, with reference to the time of their emergence from the ice of the glacial period—the less separable are they into artistic bits capable of being made into warm, sympathetic, lovable pictures with appreciable humanity in them.

Here, however, on the head waters of the Tuolumne, is a group of wild peaks on which the geologist may say that the sun has but just begun to shine, which is yet in a high degree picturesque, and in its main features so regular and evenly balanced as almost to appear conventional—one somber cluster of snow-laden peaks with gray pine-fringed granite bosses braided around its base, the whole surging free into the sky from the head of a magnificent valley, whose lofty walls are beveled away on both sides so as to embrace it all without admitting anything not strictly belonging to it. The foreground was now aflame with autumn colors, brown and purple and gold, ripe in the mellow sunshine; contrasting brightly with the deep, cobalt blue of the sky, and the black and gray, and pure, spiritual white of the rocks and glaciers. Down through the midst, the young Tuolumne was seen pouring from its crystal fountains, now resting in glassy pools as if changing back again into ice, now leaping in white cascades as if turning to snow; gliding right and left between granite bosses, then sweeping on through the smooth, meadowy levels of the valley, swaying pensively from side to side with calm, stately gestures past dipping willows and sedges, and around groves of arrowy pine; and throughout its whole eventful course, whether flowing fast or slow, singing loud or low, ever filling the landscape with spiritual animation, and manifesting the grandeur of its sources in every movement and tone.

Pursuing my lonely way down the valley, I turned again and again to gaze on the glorious picture, throwing up my arms to enclose it as in a frame. After long ages of growth in the darkness beneath the glaciers, through sunshine and storms, it seemed now to be ready and waiting for the elected artist, like yellow wheat for the reaper; and I could not help wishing that I might carry colors and brushes with me on my travels, and learn to paint. In the mean time I had to be content with photographs on my mind and sketches in my notebooks. At length, after I had rounded a precipitous headland that puts out from the west wall of the valley, every peak vanished from sight, and I pushed rapidly along the frozen meadows, over the divide between the waters of the Merced and

Tuolumne, and down through the forests that clothe the slopes of Cloud's Rest, arriving in Yosemite in due time—which, with me, is any time. And, strange to say, among the first people I met here were two artists who, with letters of introduction, were awaiting my return. They inquired whether in the course of my explorations in the adjacent mountains I had ever come upon a landscape suitable for a large painting; whereupon I began a description of the one that had so lately excited my admiration. Then, as I went on further and further into details, their faces began to glow, and I offered to guide them to it, while they declared that they would gladly follow, far or near, whithersoever I could spare the time to lead them.

Since storms might come breaking down through the fine weather at any time, burying the colors in snow and cutting off the artists' retreat, I advised getting ready at once. I led them out of the valley by the Vernal and Nevada Falls, thence over the main dividing ridge to the Big Tuolumne Meadows, by the old Mono trail, and thence along the upper Tuolumne River to its head. This was my companions' first excursion into the High Sierra, and as I was almost always alone in my mountaineering, the way that the fresh beauty was reflected in their faces made for me a novel and interesting study. They naturally were affected most of all by the colors: the intense azure of the sky, the purplish grays of the granite, the red and browns of dry meadows, and the translucent purple and crimson of huckleberry bogs; the flaming yellow of aspen groves, the silvery flashing of the streams, and the bright green and blue of the glacier lakes. But the general expression of the scenery—rocky and savage—seemed sadly disappointing; and as they threaded the forest from ridge to ridge, eagerly scanning the landscapes as they were unfolded, they said: "All this is huge and sublime, but we see nothing as yet at all available for effective pictures. Art is long, and art is limited, you know; and here are foregrounds, middle-grounds, backgrounds, all alike; bare rock-waves, woods, groves, diminutive flecks of meadow, and strips of glittering water." "Never mind," I replied, "only bide a wee, and I will show you something you will like."

At length, toward the end of the second day, the Sierra Crown began to come into view, and when we had fairly rounded the projecting headland before mentioned, the whole picture stood revealed in the flush of the alpenglow. Their enthusiasm was excited beyond bounds, and the more impulsive of the two, a young Scotchman, dashed ahead, shouting and gesticulating and tossing his arms in the air like a madman. Here, at last, was a typical alpine landscape.

After feasting awhile on the view, I proceeded to make camp in a sheltered grove a little way back from the meadow, where pine boughs could be obtained for beds, and where there was plenty of dry wood for fires, while the artists ran here and there, along the river bends and up the sides of the canyon, choosing foregrounds for sketches. After dark, when our tea was made and a rousing fire had been built, we began to make our plans. They decided to remain several days, at the least, while I concluded to make an excursion in the mean time to the untouched summit of Ritter.

It was now about the middle of October, the springtime of snow flowers. The first winter clouds had already bloomed, and the peaks were strewn with fresh crystals, without, however, affecting the climbing to any dangerous extent. And as the weather was still profoundly calm, and the distance to the foot of the mountain only a little more than a day, I felt that I was running no great risk of being storm-bound.

Mount Ritter is king of the mountains of the middle portion of the High Sierra, as Shasta of the north and Whitney of the south sections. Moreover, as far as I know, it had never been climbed. I had explored the adjacent wilderness summer after summer, but my studies thus far had never drawn me to the top of it. Its height above sea level is about 13,300 feet, and it is fenced 'round by steeply inclined glaciers, and canyons of tremendous depth and ruggedness, which render it almost inaccessible. But difficulties of this kind only exhilarate the mountaineer.

Next morning, the artists went heartily to their work and I to mine. Former experiences had given good reason to know that passionate storms, invisible as yet, might be brooding in the calm sun-gold; therefore, before bidding farewell, I warned the artists not to be alarmed should I fail to appear before a week or ten days, and advised them, in case a snowstorm should set in, to keep up big fires and shelter themselves as best they could, and on no account to become frightened and attempt to seek their way back to Yosemite alone through the drifts.

My general plan was simply this: to scale the canyon wall, cross over to the eastern flank of the range, and then make my way southward to the northern spurs of Mount Ritter in compliance with the intervening topography; for to push on directly southward from camp through the innumerable peaks and pinnacles that adorn this portion of the axis of the range, however interesting, would take too much time, besides being extremely difficult and dangerous at this time of year.

All my first day was pure pleasure; simply mountaineering indulgence, crossing the dry pathways of the ancient glaciers, tracing happy streams, and learning the habits of the birds and marmots in the groves and rocks. Before I had gone a mile from camp, I came to the foot of a white cascade that beats its way down a rugged gorge in the canyon wall, from a height of about nine hundred feet, and pours its throbbing waters into the Tuolumne. I was acquainted with its fountains, which, fortunately, lay in my course. What a fine traveling companion it proved to be, what songs it sang, and how passionately it told the mountain's own joy! Gladly I climbed along its dashing border, absorbing its divine music, and bathing from time to time in waftings of irised spray. Climbing higher, higher, new beauty came streaming on the sight: painted meadows, late-blooming gardens, peaks of rare architecture, lakes here and there, shining like silver, and glimpses of the forested middle region and the yellow lowlands far in the west. Beyond the range I saw the so-called Mono Desert, lying dreamily silent in thick purple light—a desert of heavy sun-glare beheld from a desert of ice-burnished granite. Here the waters divide, shouting in glorious enthusiasm, and falling eastward to vanish in the volcanic sands and dry sky of the Great Basin, or westward to the Great Valley of California, and thence through the Bay of San Francisco and the Golden Gate to the sea.

Passing a little way down over the summit until I had reached an elevation of about ten thousand feet, I pushed on southward toward a group of savage peaks that stand guard about Ritter on the north and west, groping my way, and dealing instinctively with every obstacle as it presented itself. Here a huge gorge would be found cutting across my path, along the dizzy edge of which I scrambled until some less precipitous point was discovered where I might safely venture to the bottom and then, selecting some feasible portion of the opposite wall, reascend with the same slow caution. Massive, flat-topped spurs alternate with the gorges, plunging abruptly from the shoulders of the snowy peaks, and planting their feet in the warm desert. These were everywhere marked and adorned with characteristic sculptures of the ancient glaciers that swept over this entire region like one vast ice-wind, and the polished surfaces produced by the ponderous flood are still so perfectly preserved that in many places the sunlight reflected from them is about as trying to the eyes as sheets of snow.

God's glacial-mills grind slowly, but they have been kept in motion long enough in California to grind sufficient soil for a glorious abundance of life, though most of the grist has been carried to the lowlands, leaving these high regions comparatively lean and bare; while the postglacial agents of erosion have not yet furnished sufficient available food over the general surface for more than a few tufts of the hardiest plants, chiefly carices and eriogonae. And it is interesting to learn in this connection that the sparseness and repressed character of the vegetation at this height is caused more by want of soil than by harshness of climate; for here and there, in sheltered hollows (countersunk beneath the general surface) into which a few rods of well ground moraine chips have been dumped, we find groves of spruce and pine thirty to forty feet high, trimmed around the edges with willow and huckleberry bushes, and oftentimes still farther by an outer ring of tall grasses, bright with lupines, larkspurs, and showy columbines, suggesting a climate by no means repressingly severe. All the streams, too, and the pools at this elevation are furnished with little gardens wherever soil can be made to lie, which, though making scarce any show at a distance, constitute charming surprises to the appreciative observer. In these bits of leafiness a few birds find grateful homes. Having no acquaintance with man, they fear no ill, and flock curiously about the stranger, almost allowing themselves to be taken in the hand.

In so wild and so beautiful a region was spent my first day, every sight and sound inspiring, leading one far out of himself, yet feeding and building up his individuality.

Now came the solemn, silent evening. Long, blue, spiky shadows crept out across the snowfields, while a rosy glow, at first scarce discernible, gradually deepened and suffused every mountaintop, flushing the glaciers and the harsh crags above them. This was the alpenglow, to me one of the most impressive of all the terrestrial manifestations of God. At the touch of this divine light, the mountains seemed to kindle to a rapt, religious consciousness, and stood hushed and waiting like devout worshipers. Just before the alpenglow began to fade, two crimson clouds came streaming across the summit like wings of flame, rendering the sublime scene yet more impressive; then came darkness and the stars.

Icy Ritter was still miles away, but I could proceed no farther that night. I found a good campground on the rim of a glacier basin about eleven thousand feet above the sea. A small lake nestles in the bottom of it, from which I got water for my tea, and a storm-beaten thicket nearby furnished abundance of resiny firewood. Somber peaks, hacked and shattered, circled halfway around the horizon, wearing a savage aspect in the gloaming, and a waterfall chanted solemnly across the lake on its way down from the foot of a glacier. The fall and the lake and the glacier were almost equally bare; while the scraggy pines anchored in the rock fissures were so dwarfed and shorn by storm winds that you might walk over their tops. In tone and aspect the scene was one of the most desolate I ever beheld. But the darkest scriptures of the mountains are illumined with bright passages of love that never fail to make themselves felt when one is alone.

I made my bed in a nook of the pine-thicket, where the branches were pressed and crinkled overhead like a roof, and bent down around the sides. These are the best bedchambers the high mountains afford—snug as squirrel nests, well ventilated, full of spicy odors, and with plenty of wind-played needles to sing one asleep. I little expected company, but, creeping in through a low side door, I found five or six birds nestling among the tassels. The night wind began to blow soon after dark; at first only a gentle breathing, but increasing toward midnight to a rough gale that fell upon my leafy roof in ragged surges like a cascade, bearing wild sounds from the crags overhead. The waterfall sang in chorus, filling the old ice fountain with its solemn roar, and seeming to increase in power as the night advanced—fit voice for such a landscape. I had to creep out many times to the fire during the night, for it was biting cold and I had no blankets. Gladly I welcomed the morning star.

The dawn in the dry, wavering air of the desert was glorious. Everything encouraged my undertaking and betokened success. There was no cloud in the sky, no storm tone in the wind. Breakfast of bread and tea was soon made. I fastened a hard, durable crust to my belt by way of provision, in case I should be compelled to pass a night on the mountaintop; then, securing the remainder of my little stock against wolves and wood rats, I set forth free and hopeful.

How glorious a greeting the sun gives the mountains! To behold this alone is worth the pains of any excursion a thousand times over. The highest peaks burned like islands in a sea of liquid shade. Then the lower peaks and spires caught the glow, and long lances of light, streaming through many a notch and pass, fell thick on the frozen meadows. The majestic form of Ritter was full in sight, and I pushed rapidly on over rounded rock bosses and pavements, my iron-shod shoes making a clanking sound, suddenly hushed now and then in rugs of *Bryanthus*, and sedgy lake margins soft as moss. Here, too, in this so-called "land of desolation," I met *Cassiope*, growing in fringes among the battered rocks. Her blossoms had faded long ago, but they were still clinging with happy memories to the evergreen sprays, and still so beautiful as to thrill every fiber of one's being. Winter and summer, you may hear her voice, the low, sweet melody of her purple bells. No evangel among all the mountain plants speaks Nature's love more plainly than *Cassiope*. Where she dwells, the redemption of the coldest solitude is complete. The very rocks and glaciers seem to feel her presence, and become imbued with her own fountain sweetness. All things were warming and awakening. Frozen rills began to flow, the marmots came out of their nests in boulder piles and climbed sunny rocks to bask, and the dun-headed sparrows were flitting about seeking their breakfasts. The lakes seen from every ridgetop were brilliantly rippled and spangled, shimmering like the thickets of the low dwarf pines. The rocks, too, seemed responsive to the vital heat—rock crystals and snow crystals thrilling alike. I strode on exhilarated, as if never more to feel fatigue, limbs moving of themselves, every sense unfolding like the thawing flowers, to take part in the new day harmony.

All along my course thus far, excepting when down in the canyons, the landscapes were mostly open to me, and expansive, at least on one side. On the left were the purple plains of Mono, reposing dreamily and warm; on the right, the near peaks springing keenly into the thin sky with more and more impressive sublimity. But these larger views were at length lost. Rugged spurs, and moraines, and huge, projecting buttresses began to shut me in. Every feature became more rigidly alpine, without, however, producing any chilling effect; for going to the mountains is like going home. We always find that the strangest objects in these fountain wilds are in some degree familiar, and we look upon them with a vague sense of having seen them before.

On the southern shore of a frozen lake, I encountered an extensive field of hard, granular snow, up which I scampered in fine tone, intending to follow it to its head, and cross the rocky spur against which it leans, hoping thus to come direct upon the base of the main Ritter peak. The surface was pitted with oval hollows, made by stones and drifted pine needles that had melted themselves into the mass by the radiation of absorbed sun heat. These afforded good footholds, but the surface curved more and more steeply at the head, and the pits became shallower and less abundant, until I found myself in danger of being shed off like avalanching snow. I persisted, however, creeping on all fours, and shuffling up the smoothest places on my back, as I had often done on burnished granite, until, after slipping several times, I was compelled to retrace my course to the bottom, and make my way around the west end of the lake, and thence up to the summit of the divide between the head waters of Rush Creek and the northernmost tributaries of the San Joaquin.

Arriving on the summit of this dividing crest, one of the most exciting pieces of pure wilderness was disclosed that I ever discovered in all my mountaineering. There, immediately in front, loomed the majestic mass of Mount Ritter, with a glacier swooping down its face nearly to my feet, then curving westward and pouring its frozen flood into a dark blue lake, whose shores were bound with precipices of crystalline snow; while a deep chasm drawn between the divide and the glacier separated the massive picture from everything else. I could see only the one sublime mountain, the one glacier, the one lake; the whole veiled with one blue shadow-rock, ice, and water close together without a single leaf or sign of life. After gazing spellbound, I began instinctively to scrutinize every notch and gorge and weathered buttress of the mountain, with reference to making the ascent. The entire front above the glacier appeared as one tremendous precipice, slightly receding at the top, and bristling with spires and pinnacles set above one another in formidable array. Massive lichen-stained battlements stood forward here and there, hacked at the top with angular notches, and separated by frosty gullies and recesses that have been veiled in shadow ever since their creation; while to right and left, as far as I could see, were huge, crumbling buttresses, offering no hope to the climber. The head of the glacier sends up a few finger-like branches through narrow couloir, but these seemed too steep and short to be available, especially as I had no ax with which to cut steps, and the numerous narrow-throated gullies down which stones and snow are avalanched seemed hopelessly steep, besides being interrupted by vertical cliffs; while the whole front was rendered still more terribly forbidding by the chill shadow and the gloomy blackness of the rocks.

Descending the divide in a hesitating mood, I picked my way across the yawning chasm at the foot and climbed out upon the glacier. There were no meadows now to cheer with their brave colors, nor could I hear the dun-headed sparrows, whose cheery notes so often relieve the silence of our highest mountains. The only sounds were the gurgling of small rills down in the veins and crevasses of the glacier, and now and then the rattling report of falling stones, with the echoes they shot out into the crisp air.

I could not distinctly hope to reach the summit from this side, yet I moved on across the glacier as if driven by fate. Contending with myself, the season is too far spent, I said, and even should I be successful, I might be stormbound on the mountain; and in the cloud darkness, with the cliffs and crevasses covered with snow, how could I escape? No; I must wait till next summer. I would only approach the mountain now, and inspect it, creep about its flanks, learn what I could of its history, holding myself ready to flee on the approach of the first storm cloud. But we little know until tried how much of the uncontrollable there is in us, urging across glaciers and torrents, and up dangerous heights, let the judgment forbid as it may.

I succeeded in gaining the foot of the cliff on the eastern extremity of the glacier, and there discovered the mouth of a narrow avalanche gully, through which I began to climb, intending to follow it as far as possible, and at least obtain some fine wild views for my pains. Its general course is oblique to the plane of the mountain face, and the metamorphic slates of which the mountain is built are cut by cleavage planes in such a way that they weather off in angular blocks, giving rise to irregular steps that greatly facilitate climbing on the sheer places. I thus made my way into a wilderness of crumbling spires and battlements, built together in bewildering combinations, and glazed in many places with a thin coating of ice, which I had to hammer off with stones. The situation was becoming gradually more perilous; but, having passed several dangerous spots, I dared not think of descending; for, so steep was the entire ascent, one would inevitably fall to the glacier in case a single misstep were made. Knowing, therefore, the tried danger beneath, I became all the more anxious concerning the developments to be made above, and began to be conscious of a vague foreboding of what actually befell; not that I was given to fear, but rather because my instincts, usually so positive and true, seemed vitiated in some way, and were leading me astray. At length, after attaining an elevation of about 12,800 feet, I found myself at the foot of a sheer drop in the bed of the avalanche channel I was tracing, which seemed absolutely to bar further progress. It was only about forty-five or fifty feet high, and somewhat roughened by fissures and projections, but these seemed so slight and insecure as footholds that I tried hard to avoid the precipice altogether by scaling the wall of the channel on either side. But, though less steep, the walls were smoother than the obstructing rock, and repeated efforts only showed that I must either go right ahead or turn back. The tried dangers beneath seemed even greater than that of the cliff in front; therefore, after scanning its face again and again, I began to scale it, picking my holds with intense caution. After gaining a point about halfway to the top, I was suddenly brought to a dead stop, with arms outspread, clinging close to the face of the rock, unable to move hand or foot either up or down. My doom appeared fixed. I must fall. There would be a moment of bewilderment, and then a lifeless rumble down the one general precipice to the glacier below.

When this final danger flashed upon me, I became nerve-shaken for the first time since setting foot on the mountains, and my mind seemed to fill with a stifling smoke. But this terrible eclipse lasted only a moment, when life blazed forth again with preternatural clearness. I seemed suddenly to become possessed of a new sense. The other self, bygone experiences, instinct, or guardian angel— call it what you will—came forward and assumed control. Then my trembling muscles became firm again, every rift and flaw in the rock was seen as through a microscope, and my limbs moved with a positiveness and precision with which I seemed to have nothing at all to do. Had I been borne aloft upon wings, my deliverance could not have been more complete.

Above this memorable spot, the face of the mountain is still more savagely hacked and torn. It is a maze of yawning chasms and gullies, in the angles of which rise beetling crags and piles of detached boulders that seem to have been gotten ready to be launched below. But the strange influx of strength I had received seemed inexhaustible. I found a way without effort, and soon stood upon the topmost crag in the blessed light.

How truly glorious the landscape circled around this noble summit—giant mountains, valleys innumerable, glaciers and meadows, rivers and lakes, with the wide blue sky bent tenderly over them all. But in my first hour of freedom from that terrible shadow, the sunlight in which I was laying seemed all in all.

Looking southward along the axis of the range, the eye is first caught by a row of exceedingly sharp and slender spires, which rise openly to a height of about a thousand feet, above a series of short, residual glaciers that lean back against their bases; their fantastic sculpture and the unrelieved sharpness with which they spring out of the ice rendering them peculiarly wild and striking. These are "The Minarets." Beyond them you behold a sublime wilderness of mountains, their snowy summits towering together in crowded abundance, peak beyond peak, swelling higher, higher as they sweep on southward, until the culminating point of the range is reached on Mount Whitney, near the head of the Kern River, at an elevation of nearly 14,700 feet above the level of the sea.

Westward, the general flank of the range is seen flowing sublimely away from the sharp summits, in smooth undulations; a sea of huge, gray, granite waves dotted with lakes and meadows, and fluted with stupendous canyons that grow steadily deeper as they recede in the distance. Below this gray region lies the dark forest zone, broken here and there by upswelling ridges and domes; and yet beyond lies a yellow, hazy belt, marking the broad plain of the San Joaquin, bounded on its farther side by the blue mountains of the coast.

Turning now to the northward, there in the immediate foreground is the glorious Sierra Crown, with Cathedral Peak, a temple of marvelous architecture, a few degrees to the left of it; the gray, massive form of Mammoth Mountain to the right; while mounts Ord, Gibbs, Dana, Conness, Tower Peak, Castle Peak, Silver Mountain, and a host of noble companions, as yet nameless, make a sublime show along the axis of the range.

Eastward, the whole region seems a land of desolation covered with beautiful light. The torrid volcanic basin of Mono, with its one bare lake fourteen miles long; Owen's Valley and the broad lava table land at its head, dotted with craters, and the massive Inyo Range, rivaling even the Sierra in height; these are spread, map-like, beneath you, with countless ranges beyond, passing and overlapping one another and fading on the glowing horizon.

At a distance of less than three thousand feet below the summit of Mount Ritter you may find tributaries of the San Joaquin and Owen's rivers, bursting forth from the ice and snow of the glaciers that load its flanks; while a little to the north of here are found the highest affluents of the Tuolumne and Merced. Thus, the fountains of four of the principal rivers of California are within a radius of four or five miles.

Lakes are seen gleaming in all sorts of places—round, or oval, or square, like very mirrors; others narrow and sinuous, drawn close around the peaks like silver zones, the highest reflecting only rocks, snow, and the sky. But neither these nor the glaciers, nor the bits of brown meadow and moorland that occur here and there, are large enough to make any marked impression upon the mighty wilderness of mountains. The eye, rejoicing in its freedom, roves about the vast expanse, yet returns again and again to the fountain peaks. Perhaps some one of the multitude excites special attention, some gigantic castle with turret and battlement, or some Gothic cathedral more abundantly spired than Milan's. But, generally, when looking for the first time from an all-embracing standpoint like this, the inexperienced observer is oppressed by the incomprehensible grandeur, variety, and abundance of the mountains rising shoulder to shoulder beyond the reach of vision; and it is only after they have been studied one by one, long and lovingly, that their far-reaching harmonies become manifest. Then, penetrate the wilderness where you may, the main telling features, to which all the surrounding topography is subordinate, are quickly perceived, and the most complicated clusters of peaks stand revealed harmoniously correlated and fashioned like works of art—eloquent monuments of the ancient ice rivers that brought them into relief from the general mass of the range. The canyons, too, some of them a mile deep, mazing wildly through the mighty host of mountains, however lawless and ungovernable at first sight they appear, are at length recognized as the necessary effects of causes which followed each other in harmonious sequence—Nature's poems carved on tables of stone—the simplest and most emphatic of her glacial compositions.

Could we have been here to observe during the glacial period, we should have overlooked a wrinkled ocean of ice as continuous as that now covering the landscapes of Greenland; filling every valley and canyon with only the tops of the fountain peaks rising darkly above the rock-encumbered ice waves like islets in a stormy sea—

those islets the only hints of the glorious landscapes now smiling in the sun. Standing here in the deep, brooding silence all the wilderness seems motionless, as if the work of creation were done. But in the midst of this outer steadfastness we know there is incessant motion and change. Ever and anon, avalanches are falling from yonder peaks. These cliff-bound glaciers, seemingly wedged and immovable, are flowing like water and grinding the rocks beneath them. The lakes are lapping their granite shores and wearing them away, and every one of these rills and young rivers is fretting the air into music, and carrying the mountains to the plains. Here are the roots of all the life of the valleys, and here more simply than elsewhere is the eternal flux of nature manifested. Ice changing to water, lakes to meadows, and mountains to plains. And while we thus contemplate nature's methods of landscape creation, and, reading the records she has carved on the rocks, reconstruct, however imperfectly, the landscapes of the past, we also learn that as these we now behold have succeeded those of the preglacial age, so they in turn are withering and vanishing to be succeeded by others yet unborn.

But in the midst of these fine lessons and landscapes, I had to remember that the sun was wheeling far to the west, while a new way down the mountain had to be discovered to some point on the timber line where I could have a fire; for I had not even burdened myself with a coat. I first scanned the western spurs, hoping some way might appear through which I might reach the northern glacier, and cross its snout; or pass around the lake into which it flows, and thus strike my morning track. This route was soon sufficiently unfolded to show that, if practicable at all, it would require so much time that reaching camp that night would be out of the question. I therefore scrambled back eastward, descending the southern slopes obliquely at the same time. Here the crags seemed less formidable, and the head of a glacier that flows northeast came in sight, which I determined to follow as far as possible, hoping thus to make my way to the foot of the peak on the east side, and thence across the intervening canyons and ridges to camp.

The inclination of the glacier is quite moderate at the head, and, as the sun had softened the névé, I made safe and rapid progress, running and sliding, and keeping up a sharp outlook for crevasses. About half a mile from the head, there is an ice cascade, where the glacier pours over a sharp declivity and is shattered into massive blocks separated by deep, blue fissures. To thread my way through the slippery mazes of this crevassed portion seemed impossible, and I endeavored to avoid it by climbing off to the shoulder of the mountain. But the slopes rapidly steepened and at length fell away in sheer precipices, compelling a return to the ice. Fortunately, the day had been warm enough to loosen the ice crystals so as to admit of hollows being dug in the rotten portions of the blocks, thus enabling me to pick my way with far less difficulty than I had anticipated. Continuing down over the snout, and along the left lateral moraine, was only a confident saunter, showing that the ascent of the mountain by way of this glacier is easy, provided one is armed with an ax to cut steps here and there.

The lower end of the glacier was beautifully waved and barred by the outcropping edges of the bedded ice layers, which represent the annual snowfalls and, to some extent, the irregularities of structure caused by the weathering of the walls of crevasses, and by separate snowfalls which have been followed by rain, hail, thawing and freezing, etc. Small rills were gliding and swirling over the melting surface with a smooth, oily appearance, in channels of pure ice—their quick, compliant movements contrasting most impressively with the rigid, invisible flow of the glacier itself, on whose back they all were riding.

Night drew near before I reached the eastern base of the mountain, and my camp lay many a rugged mile to the north, but ultimate success was assured. It was now only a matter of endurance and ordinary mountain-craft. The sunset was, if possible, yet more beautiful than that of the day before. The Mono landscape seemed to be fairly saturated with warm, purple light. The peaks marshaled along the summit were in shadow, but through every notch and pass streamed vivid sun-fire, soothing and irradiating their rough, black angles, while companies of small, luminous clouds hovered above them like very angels of light.

Darkness came on, but I found my way by the trends of the canyons and the peaks projected against the sky. All excitement died with the light, and then I was weary. But the joyful sound of the waterfall across the lake was heard at last, and soon the stars were seen reflected in the lake itself. Taking my bearings from these, I discovered the little pine thicket in which my nest was, and then I had a rest such as only a tired mountaineer may enjoy. After lying loose and lost for a while, I made a sunrise fire, went down to the lake, dashed water on my head, and dipped a cupful for tea. The revival brought about by bread and tea was as complete as the exhaustion from excessive enjoyment and toil. Then I crept beneath the pine tassels to bed. The wind was frosty and the fire burned low, but my sleep was nonetheless sound, and the evening constellations had swept far to the west before I awoke.

After thawing and resting in the morning sunshine, I sauntered home—that is, back to the Tuolumne camp—bearing away toward a cluster of peaks that hold the fountain snows of one of the north tributaries of Rush Creek. Here I discovered a group of beautiful glacier lakes, nestled together in a grand amphitheater. Toward evening, I crossed the divide separating the Mono waters from those of the Tuolumne, and entered the glacier basin that now holds the fountain snows of the stream that forms the upper Tuolumne cascades. This stream I traced down through its many dells and gorges, meadows and bogs, reaching the brink of the main Tuolumne at dusk.

A loud whoop for the artists was answered again and again. Their campfire came in sight, and half an hour afterward I was with them. They seemed unreasonably glad to see me. I had been absent only three days; nevertheless, though the weather was fine, they had already been weighing chances as to whether I would ever return, and trying to decide whether they should wait longer or begin to seek their way back to the lowlands. Now their curious troubles were over. They packed their precious sketches, and next morning we set out homeward bound, and in two days entered the Yosemite Valley from the north by way of Indian Canyon.

A Windstorm in the Forest

The mountain winds, like the dew and rain, sunshine and snow, are measured and bestowed with love on the forests to develop their strength and beauty. However restricted the scope of other forest influences, that of the winds is universal. The snow bends and trims the upper forests every winter, the lightning strikes a single tree here and there, while avalanches mow down thousands at a swoop as a gardener trims out a bed of flowers. But the winds go to every tree, fingering every leaf and branch and furrowed bole; not one is forgotten; the mountain pine towering with outstretched arms on the rugged buttresses of the icy peaks, the lowliest and most retiring tenant of the dells; they seek and find them all, caressing them tenderly, bending them in lusty exercise, stimulating their growth, plucking off a leaf or limb as required, or removing an entire tree or grove, now whispering and cooing through the branches like a sleepy child, now roaring like the ocean; the winds blessing the forests, the forests the winds, with ineffable beauty and harmony as the sure result.

After one has seen pines six feet in diameter bending like grasses before a mountain gale, and ever and anon some giant falling with a crash that shakes the hills, it seems astonishing that any, save the lowest thickset trees, could ever have found a period sufficiently stormless to establish themselves; or, once established, that they should not, sooner or later, have been blown down. But when the storm is over, and we behold the same forests tranquil again, towering fresh and unscathed in erect majesty, and consider what centuries of storms have fallen upon them since they were first planted—hail, to break the tender seedlings; lightning, to scorch and shatter; snow, winds, and avalanches, to crush and overwhelm—while the manifest result of all this wild storm culture is the glorious perfection we behold; then faith in Nature's forestry is established, and we cease to deplore the violence of her most destructive gales, or of any other storm implement whatsoever.

There are two trees in the Sierra forests that are never blown down, so long as they continue in sound health. These are the juniper and the dwarf pine of the summit peaks. Their stiff, crooked roots grip the storm-beaten ledges like eagles' claws, while their lithe, cord-like branches bend round compliantly, offering but slight holds for winds, however violent. The other alpine conifers —the needle pine, mountain pine, two-leaved pine, and hemlock spruce—are never thinned out by this agent to any destructive extent, on account of their admirable toughness and the closeness of their growth. In general the same is true of the giants of the lower zones. The kingly sugar pine, towering aloft to a height of more than two hundred feet, offers a fine mark to storm winds; but it is not densely foliaged, and its long, horizontal arms swing 'round compliantly in the blast, like tresses of green, fluent algae in a brook; while the silver firs in most places keep their ranks well together in united strength. The yellow or silver pine is more frequently overturned than any other tree on the Sierra, because its leaves and branches form a larger mass in proportion to its height, while in many places it is planted sparsely, leaving open lanes through which storms may enter with full force. Furthermore, because it is distributed along the lower portion of the range, which was the first to be left bare on the breaking up of the ice sheet at the close of the glacial winter, the soil it is growing upon has been longer exposed to postglacial weathering, and consequently is in a more crumbling, decayed condition than the fresher soils farther up the range, and therefore offers a less secure anchorage for the roots.

While exploring the forest zones of Mount Shasta, I discovered the path of a hurricane strewn with thousands of pines of this species. Great and small had been uprooted or wrenched off by sheer force, making a clean gap, like that made by a snow avalanche. But hurricanes capable of doing this class of work are rare in the Sierra, and when we have explored the forests from one extremity of the range to the other, we are compelled to believe that they are the most beautiful on the face of the earth, however we may regard the agents that have made them so.

There is always something deeply exciting, not only in the sounds of winds in the woods, which exert more or less influence over every mind, but in their varied waterlike flow as manifested by the movements of the trees, especially those of the conifers. By no other trees are they rendered so extensively and impressively visible, not even by the lordly tropic palms or tree ferns responsive to the gentlest breeze. The waving of a forest of the giant sequoias is indescribably impressive and sublime, but the pines seem to me the best interpreters of winds. They are mighty waving goldenrods, ever in tune, singing and writing wind music all their long century lives. Little, however, of this noble tree waving and tree music will you see or hear in the strictly alpine portion of the forests. The burly juniper, whose girth sometimes more than equals its height, is about as rigid as the rocks on which it grows. The slender lash-like sprays of the dwarf pine stream out in wavering ripples, but the tallest and slenderest are far too unyielding to wave even in the heaviest gales. They only shake in quick, short vibrations. The hemlock spruce, however, and the mountain pine, and some of the tallest thickets of the two-leaved species bow in storms with considerable scope and gracefulness. But it is only in the lower and middle zones that the meeting of winds and woods is to be seen in all its grandeur.

One of the most beautiful and exhilarating storms I ever enjoyed in the Sierra occurred in December 1874, when I happened to be exploring one of the tributary valleys of the Yuba River. The sky and the ground and the trees had been thoroughly rain-washed and were dry again. The day was intensely pure, one of those incomparable bits of California winter, warm and balmy and full of white, sparkling sunshine, redolent of all the purest influences of the spring and at the same time enlivened with one of the most bracing windstorms conceivable. Instead of camping out, as I usually do, I then chanced to be stopping at the house of a friend. But when the storm began to sound, I lost no time in pushing out into the woods to enjoy it. For, on such occasions, nature has always something rare to show us, and the danger to life and limb is hardly greater than one would experience crouching deprecatingly beneath a roof.

It was still early morning when I found myself fairly adrift. Delicious sunshine came pouring over the hills, lighting the tops of the pines and setting free a steam of summery fragrance that contrasted strangely with the wild tones of the storm. The air was mottled with pine tassels and bright green plumes that went flashing past in the sunlight like birds pursued. But there was not the slightest dustiness, nothing less pure than leaves, and ripe pollen, and flecks of withered bracken and moss. I heard trees falling for hours at the rate of one every two or three minutes; some uprooted, partly on account of the loose, water-soaked condition of the ground; others broken straight across, where some weakness caused by fire had determined the spot. The gestures of the various trees made a delightful study. Young sugar pines, light and feathery as squirrel tails, were bowing almost to the ground, while the grand old patriarchs, whose massive boles had been tried in a hundred storms, waved solemnly above them, their long, arching branches streaming fluently on the gale, and every needle thrilling and ringing and shedding off keen lances of light like a diamond. The Douglas spruces, with long sprays drawn out in level tresses, and needles massed in a gray, shimmering glow, presented a most striking appearance as they stood in bold relief along the hilltops. The madronos in the dells, with their red bark and large glossy leaves tilted every way, reflected the sunshine in throbbing spangles like those one so often sees on the rippled surface of a glacier lake. But the silver pines were now the most impressively beautiful of all. Colossal spires 200 feet in height waved like supple goldenrods, chanting and bowing low as if in worship, while the whole mass of their long, tremulous foliage was kindled into one continuous blaze of white sun-fire. The force of the gale was such that the most steadfast monarch of them all rocked down to its roots with a motion plainly perceptible when one leaned against it. Nature was holding high festival, and every fiber of the most rigid giants thrilled with glad excitement.

I drifted on through the midst of this passionate music and motion, across many a glen, from ridge to ridge, often halting in the lee of a rock for shelter, or to gaze and listen. Even when the grand anthem had swelled to its highest pitch, I could distinctly hear the varying tones of individual trees, spruce, and fir, and pine, and leafless oak—and even the infinitely gentle rustle of the withered grasses at my feet. Each was expressing itself in its own way—singing its own song and making its own peculiar gestures—manifesting a richness of variety to be found in no other forest I have yet seen. The coniferous woods of Canada, and the Carolinas, and Florida, are made up of trees that resemble one another about as nearly as blades of grass, and grow close together in much the same way. Coniferous trees, in general, seldom possess individual character, such as is manifest among oaks and elms. But the California forests are made up of a greater number of distinct species than any other in the world. And in them we find, not only a marked differentiation into special groups, but also a marked individuality in almost every tree, giving rise to storm effects indescribably glorious.

Toward midday, after a long, tingling scramble through copses of hazel and *Ceanothus*, I gained the summit of the highest ridge in the neighborhood; and then it occurred to me that it would be a fine thing to climb one of the trees to obtain a wider outlook and get my ear close to the Aeolian music of its topmost needles. But under the circumstances, the choice of a tree was a serious matter. One whose instep was not very strong seemed in danger of being blown down, or of being struck by others in case they should fall; another was branchless to a considerable height above the ground, and at the same time too large to be grasped with arms and legs in climbing; while others were not favorably situated for clear views. After cautiously casting about, I made choice of the tallest of a group of Douglas spruces that were growing close together like a tuft of grass, no one of which seemed likely to fall unless all the rest fell with it. Though comparatively young, they were about 100 feet high, and their lithe, brushy tops were rocking and swirling in wild ecstasy. Being accustomed to climb trees in making botanical studies, I experienced no difficulty in reaching the top of this one, and never before did I enjoy so noble an exhilaration of motion. The slender tops fairly flapped and swished in the passionate torrent, bending and swirling backward and forward, round and round, tracing indescribable combinations of vertical and horizontal curves, while I clung with muscles firm braced, like a bobolink on a reed.

In its widest sweeps, my tree-top described an arc of from twenty to thirty degrees, but I felt sure of its elastic temper, having seen others of the same species still more severely tried—bent almost to the ground indeed, in heavy snows without breaking a fiber. I was therefore safe, and free to take the wind into my pulses and enjoy the excited forest from my superb outlook. The view from here must be extremely beautiful in any weather. Now my eye roved over the piney hills and dales as over fields of waving grain, and felt the light running in ripples and broad swelling undulations across the valleys from ridge to ridge, as the shining foliage was stirred by corresponding waves of air. Oftentimes these waves of reflected light would break up suddenly into a kind of beaten foam, and again, after chasing one another in regular order, they would seem to bend forward in concentric curves, and disappear on some hillside, like sea waves on a shelving shore. The quantity of light reflected from the bent needles was so great as to make whole groves appear as if covered with snow, while the black shadows beneath the trees greatly enhanced the effect of the silvery splendor.

Excepting only the shadows, there was nothing somber in all this wild sea of pines. On the contrary, notwithstanding this was the winter season, the colors were remarkably beautiful. The shafts of the pine and *Libocedrus* were brown and purple, and most of the foliage was well tinged with yellow; the laurel groves, with the pale undersides of their leaves turned upward, made masses of gray; and then there was many a dash of chocolate color from clumps of manzanita, and jet of vivid crimson from the bark of the madronos, while the ground on the hillsides, appearing here and there through openings between the groves, displayed masses of pale purple and brown.

The sounds of the storm corresponded gloriously with this wild exuberance of light and motion. The profound bass of the naked branches and boles booming like waterfalls; the quick, tense vibrations of the pine needles, now rising to a shrill, whistling hiss, now falling to a silky murmur; the rustling of laurel groves in the dells, and the keen metallic click of leaf on leaf—all this was heard in easy analysis when the attention was calmly bent.

The varied gestures of the multitude were seen to fine advantage, so that one could recognize the different species at a distance of several miles by this means alone, as well as by their forms and colors, and the way they reflected the light. All seemed strong and comfortable, as if really enjoying the storm, while responding to its most enthusiastic greetings. We hear much nowadays concerning the universal struggle for existence, but no struggle in the common meaning of the word was manifest here; no recognition of danger by any tree; no deprecation; but rather an invincible gladness as remote from exultation as from fear.

I kept my lofty perch for hours, frequently closing my eyes to enjoy the music by itself, or to feast quietly on the delicious fragrance that was streaming past. The fragrance of the woods was less marked than that produced during warm rain, when so many balsamic buds and leaves are steeped like tea; but, from the chafing of resiny branches against each other, and the incessant attrition of myriad needles, the gale was spiced to a very tonic degree. And besides the fragrance from these local sources, there were traces of scents brought from afar. For this wind came first from the sea, rubbing against its fresh, briny waves, then distilled through the redwoods, threading rich ferny gulches, and spreading itself in broad undulating currents over many a flower-enameled ridge of the coast mountains, then across the golden plains, up the purple foothills, and into these piney woods with the varied incense gathered by the way.

Winds are advertisements of all they touch, however much or little we may be able to read them; telling their wanderings even by their scents alone. Mariners detect the flowery perfume of land winds far at sea, and sea winds carry the fragrance of dulse and tangle far inland, where it is quickly recognized, though mingled with the scents of a thousand land flowers. As an illustration of this, I may tell here that I breathed sea air on the Firth of Forth in Scotland, while a boy; then was taken to Wisconsin, where I remained nineteen years; then, without in all this time having breathed one breath of the sea, I walked quietly, alone, from the middle of the Mississippi Valley to the Gulf of Mexico, on a botanical excursion, and while in Florida, far from the coast, my attention wholly bent on the splendid tropical vegetation about me, I suddenly recognized a sea breeze, as it came sifting through the palmettos and blooming vine-tangles, which at once awakened and set free a thousand dormant associations, and made me a boy again in Scotland, as if all the intervening years had been annihilated.

Most people like to look at mountain rivers, and bear them in mind, but few care to look at the winds, though far more beautiful and sublime, and though they become at times about as visible as flowing water. When the north winds in winter are making upward sweeps over the curving summits of the High Sierra, the fact is sometimes published with flying snow-banners a mile long. Those portions of the winds thus embodied can scarce be wholly invisible, even to the darkest imagination. And when we look around over an agitated forest, we may see something of the wind that stirs it, by its effects upon the trees. Yonder it descends in a rush of water-like ripples and sweeps over the bending pines from hill to hill. Nearer, we see detached plumes and leaves, now speeding by on level currents, now whirling in eddies, or, escaping over the edges of the whirls, soaring aloft on grand, upswelling domes of air, or tossing on flame-like crests. Smooth, deep currents, cascades, falls, and swirling eddies sing around every tree and leaf, and over all the varied topography of the region with telling changes of form, like mountain rivers conforming to the features of their channels.

After tracing the Sierra streams from their fountains to the plains, marking where they bloom white in falls, glide in crystal plumes, surge gray and foam-filled in boulder-choked gorges, and slip through the woods in long, tranquil reaches after thus learning their language and forms in detail, we may at length hear them chanting all together in one grand anthem, and comprehend them all in clear inner vision, covering the range like lace. But even this spectacle is far less sublime and not a whit more substantial than what we may behold of these storm-streams of air in the mountain woods.

We all travel the Milky Way together, trees and men, but it never occurred to me until this storm day, while swinging in the wind, that trees are travelers in the ordinary sense. They make many journeys, not extensive ones it is true; but our own little journeys, away and back again, are only little more than tree wavings—many of them not so much.

When the storm began to abate, I dismounted and sauntered down through the calming woods. The storm tones died away, and, turning toward the east, I beheld the countless hosts of the forests hushed and tranquil, towering above one another on the slopes of the hills like a devout audience. The setting sun filled them with amber light and seemed to say, while they listened, "My peace I give unto you."

As I gazed on the impressive scene, all the so-called ruin of the storm was forgotten, and never before did these noble woods appear so fresh, so joyous, so immortal.

A Yosemite Earthquake

At half-past two o'clock of a moonlit morning in March, I was awakened by a tremendous earthquake, and though I had never before enjoyed a storm of this sort, the strange thrilling motion could not be mistaken, and I ran out of my cabin, both glad and frightened, shouting, "A noble earthquake! A noble earthquake!" feeling sure I was going to learn something. The shocks were so violent and varied, and succeeded one another so closely, that I had to balance myself carefully in walking as if on the deck of a ship among waves, and it seemed impossible that the high cliffs of the Valley could escape being shattered. In particular, I feared that the sheer-fronted Sentinel Rock, towering above my cabin, would be shaken down, and I took shelter back of a large yellow pine, hoping that it might protect me from at least the smaller outbounding boulders. For a minute or two the shocks became more and more violent—flashing horizontal thrusts mixed with a few twists and battering, explosive, upheaving jolts,—as if Nature were wrecking her Yosemite temple, and getting ready to build a still better one.

I was now convinced before a single boulder had fallen that earthquakes were the talus-makers and positive proof soon came. It was a calm moonlight night, and no sound was heard for the first minute or so, save low, muffled, underground, bubbling rumblings, and the whispering and rustling of the agitated trees, as if Nature were holding her breath. Then, suddenly, out of the strange silence and strange motion there came a tremendous roar. The Eagle Rock on the south wall, about a half a mile up the Valley, gave way and I saw it falling in thousands of the great boulders I had so long been studying, pouring to the Valley floor in a free curve luminous from friction, making a terribly sublime spectacle—an arc of glowing, passionate fire, fifteen hundred feet span, as true in form and as serene in beauty as a rainbow in the midst of the stupendous, roaring rock-storm. The sound was so tremendously deep and broad and earnest, the whole earth like a living creature seemed to have at last found a voice and to be calling to her sister planets. In trying to tell something of the size of this awful sound it seems to me that if all the thunder of all the storms had ever heard were condensed into one roar it would not equal this rock-roar at the birth of a mountain talus. Think, then, of the roar that arose to heaven at the simultaneous birth of all the thousands of ancient cañon-taluses throughout the length and breadth of the Range!

The first severe shocks were soon over, and eager to examine the new-born talus I ran up the Valley in the moonlight and climbed upon it before the huge blocks, after their fiery flight, had come to complete rest. They were slowly settling into their places, chafing, grating against one another, groaning, and whispering; but no motion was visible except in a stream of small fragments pattering down the face of the cliff. A cloud of dust particles, lighted by the moon, floated out across the whole breadth of the Valley, forming a ceiling that lasted until after sunrise, and the air was filled with the odor of crushed Douglas spruces from a grove that had been mowed down and mashed like weeds.

After the ground began to calm I ran across the meadow to the river to see in what direction it was flowing and was glad to find that *down* the Valley was still down. Its waters were muddy from portions of its banks having given way, but it was flowing around its curves and over its ripples and shallows with ordinary tones and gestures. The mud would soon be cleared away and the raw slips on the banks would be the only visible record of the shaking it suffered.

The Upper Yosemite Fall, glowing white in the moonlight, seemed to know nothing of the earthquake, manifesting no change in form or voice, as far as I could see or hear.

After a second startling shock, about half-past three o'clock, the ground continued to tremble gently, and smooth, hollow rumbling sounds, not always distinguishable from the rounded, bumping, explosive tones of the falls, came from deep in the mountains in a northern direction.

The few Indians fled from their huts to the middle of the Valley, fearing that angry spirits were trying to kill them; and, as I afterward learned, most of the Yosemite tribe, who were spending the winter at their village on Bull Creek forty miles away, were so terrified that they ran into the river and washed themselves,— getting themselves clean enough to say their prayers, I suppose, or to die. I asked Dick, one of the Indians with whom I was acquainted, "What made the ground shake and jump so much?" He only shook his head and said, "No good. No good," and looked appealingly to me to give him hope that his life was to be spared.

In the morning I found the few white settlers assembled in front of the old Hutchings Hotel comparing notes and meditating light to the lowlands, seemingly as sorely frightened as the Indians. Shortly after sunrise a low, blunt, muffled rumbling, like distant thunder, was followed by another series of shocks, which, though not nearly so severe as the first, made the cliffs and domes tremble like jelly, and the big pines and oaks thrill and swish and wave their branches with startling effect. Then the talkers were suddenly hushed, and the solemnity on their faces was sublime. One in particular of these winter neighbors, a somewhat speculative thinker with whom I had open conversed, was a firm believer in the cataclysmic origin of the Valley; and I now jokingly remarked that his wild tumble-down-and-engulfment hypothesis might soon be proved, since these underground rumblings and shakings might be the forerunners of another Yosemite-making cataclysm, which would perhaps double the depth of the Valley by swallowing the floor, leaving the ends of the roads and trails dangling three or four thousand feet in the air. Just then came the third series of shocks, and it was fine to see how awfully silent and solemn he became. His belief in the existence of a mysterious abyss, into which the suspended floor of the Valley and all the domes and battlements of the walls might at any moment go roaring down, mightily troubled him. To diminish his fears and laugh him into something like reasonable faith, I said, "Come, cheer up; smile a little and clap your hands, now that kind Mother Earth is trotting us on her knee to amuse us and make us good." But the well-meant joke seemed irreverent and utterly failed, as if only prayerful terror could rightly belong to the wild beauty-making business. Even after all the heavier shocks were over I could do nothing to reassure him, on the contrary, he handed me the keys of his little store to keep, saying that with a companion of like mind he was going to the lowlands to stay until the fate of poor, trembling Yosemite was settled. In vain I rallied them on their fears, calling attention to the strength of the granite walls of our Valley home, the very best and solidest masonry in the world, and less likely to collapse and sink than the sedimentary lowlands to which they were looking for safety; and saying that in any case they sometime would have to die, and so grand a burial was not to be slighted. But they were too seriously panic-stricken to get comfort from anything I could say.

During the third severe shock the trees were so violently shaken that the birds flew out with frightened cries. In particular, I noticed two robins flying in terror from a leafless oak, the branches of which swished and quivered as if struck by a heavy battering-ram. Exceedingly interesting were the flashing and quivering of the elastic needles of the pines in the sunlight and the waving up and down of the branches while the trunks stood rigid. There was no swaying, waving or swirling as in wind-storms, but quick, quivering jerks, and at times the heavy tasseled branches moved as if they had all been pressed down against the trunk and suddenly let go, to spring up and vibrate until they came to rest again. Only the owls seemed to be undisturbed. Before the rumbling echoes had died away a hollow-voiced owl began to hoot in philosophical tranquillity from near the edge of the new talus as if nothing extraordinary had occurred, although, perhaps, he was curious to know what all the noise was about. His "hoot-too-hoot-too-whoo" might have meant, "what's a' the steer, kimmer?"

It was long before the Valley found perfect rest. The rocks trembled more or less every day for over two months, and I kept a bucket of water on my table to learn what I could of the movements. The blunt thunder in the depths of the mountains was usually followed by sudden jarring, horizontal thrusts from the northward, often succeeded by twisting, upjolting movements. More than a month after the first great shock, when I was standing on a fallen tree up the Valley near Lamon's winter cabin, I heard a distinct bubbling thunder from the direction of Tenaya Cañon Carlo, a large intelligent St. Bernard dog standing beside me seemed greatly astonished, and looked intently in that direction with mouth open and uttered a low *Wouf!* as if saying, "What's that?" He must have known that it was not thunder, though like it. The air was perfectly still, not the faintest breath of wind perceptible, and a fine, mellow, sunny hush pervaded everything, in the midst of which came that subterranean thunder. Then, while we gazed and listened, came the corresponding shocks, distinct as if some mighty hand had shaken the ground. After the sharp horizontal jars died away, they were followed by a gentle rocking and undulating of the ground so distinct that Carlo looked at the log on which he was standing to see who was shaking it. It was the season of flooded meadows and the pools about me, calm as sheets of glass, were suddenly thrown into low ruffling waves.

Judging by its effects, this Yosemite, or Inyo earthquake, as it is sometimes called, was gentle as compared with the one that gave rise to the grand talus system of the Range and did so much for the cañon scenery. Nature, usually so deliberate in her operations, then created, as we have seen, a new set of features, simply by giving the mountains a shake—changing not only the high peaks and cliffs, but the streams. As soon as these rock avalanches fell the streams began to sing new songs; for in many places thousands of boulders were hurled into their channels, roughening and half-damming them, compelling the waters to surge and roar in rapids where before they glided smoothly. Some of the streams were completely dammed; driftwood, leaves, etc., gradually filling the interstices between the boulders, thus giving rise to lakes and level reaches;

and these again, after being gradually filled in, were changed to meadows, through which the streams are now silently meandering; while at the same time some of the taluses took the places of old meadows and groves. Thus rough places were made smooth, and smooth places rough. But, on the whole, by what at first sight seemed pure confounded confusion and ruin, the landscapes were enriched; for gradually every talus was covered with groves and gardens, and made a finely proportioned and ornamental base for the cliffs. In this work of beauty, every boulder is prepared and measured and put in its place more thoughtfully than are the stones of temples. If for a moment you are inclined to regard these taluses as mere draggled, chaotic dumps, climb to the top of one of them, and run down without any haggling, puttering hesitation, boldly jumping from boulder to boulder with even speed. You will then find your feet playing a tune, and quickly discover the music and poetry of these magnificent rock piles—a fine lesson; and all Nature's wildness tells the same story—the shocks and outbursts of earthquakes, volcanoes, geysers, roaring, thundering waves and floods, the silent uprush of sap in plants, storms of every sort—each and all are the orderly beauty-making love-beats of Nature's heart.

Yosemite Falls at Midnight

To Mrs. Ezra S. Carr

<small>MIDNIGHT, YOSEMITE
APRIL 3, 1871</small>

Oh, Mrs. Carr, that you could be here to mingle in this night-noon glory! I am in the upper Yosemite Falls and can hardly calm to write, but from my first baptism hours ago, you have been so present that I must try to fix you a written thought.

In the afternoon I came up the mountain here with a blanket and a piece of bread to spend the night in prayer among the spouts of this fall. But what can I say more than wish again that you might expose your soul to the rays of this heaven?

Silver from the moon illumines this glorious creation which we term "falls," and has laid a magnificent double prismatic bow at its base.

The tissue of the fall is delicately filmed on the outside like the substance of spent clouds, and the stars shine dimly through it. In the solid shafted body of the fall is a vast number of passing caves, black and deep, with close, white, convolving spray for sills and shooting-comet sheaves above and down their sides, like lime crystals in a cave. And every atom of the magnificent being, from the thin, silvery crest that does not dim the stars to the inner arrowy hardened shafts that strike onward like thunderbolts in sound and energy, all is life and spirit: every bolt and spray feels the hand of God. Oh, the music that is blessing me now! The sun of last week has given the grandest notes of all the yearly anthem.

I said that I was going to stop here until morning and pray a whole blessed night with the falls and the moon, but I am too wet and must go down. An hour or two ago I went out somehow on a little seam that extends along the wall behind the falls. I suppose I was in a trance, but I can positively say that I was in the body, for it is sorely battered and wetted. As I was gazing past the thin edge of the fall and away beneath the column to the brow of the rock, some heavy splashes of water struck me, driven hard against the wall. Suddenly I was darkened, down came a section of the outside tissue composed of spent comets. I crouched low, holding my breath, and anchored to some angular flakes of rock, took my baptism with moderately good faith.

When I dared to look up after the swaying column admitted light, I pounced behind a piece of ice and the wall which was wedging tight, and I no longer feared being washed off, and steady moonbeams slanting past the arching meteors gave me confidence to escape to this snug place where McChesney and I slept one night, where I have a fire to dry my socks. This rock shell, extending behind the falls, is about five hundred feet above the base of the fall on the perpendicular rock face.

How little do we know of ourselves, of our profoundest attractions and repulsions, of our spiritual affinities! How interesting does man become considered in his relations to the spirit of this rock and water! How significant does every atom of our world become amid the influences of those beings unseen, spiritual, angelic mountaineers that so throng these pure mansions of crystal foam and purple granite.

I cannot refrain from speaking to this little bush at my side and to the spray drops that come to my paper and to the individual sands of the slopelet I am sitting upon. Ruskin says that the idea of foulness is essentially connected with what he calls dead, unorganized matter. How cordially I disbelieve him tonight, and were he to dwell awhile among the powers of these mountains he would forget all dictionary differences betwixt the clean and the unclean, and he would lose all memory and meaning of the diabolical sin-begotten term foulness.

Well, I must go down. I am disregarding all of the doctors' physiology in sitting here in this universal moisture. Farewell to you, and to all the beings about us. I shall have a glorious walk down the mountain in this thin, white light, over the open brows grayed with *Selaginella* and through the thick black shadow caves in the live oaks, all stuck full of snowy lances of moonlight.

[John Muir]

Nut Time in Squirrelville

TO MRS. EZRA S. CARR
SQUIRRELVILLE, SEQUOIA CO.
NUT TIME

Dear Mrs. Carr:
Do behold the King in his glory, King Sequoia! Behold! Behold!
seems all I can say. Some time ago I left all for Sequoia and have
been and am at his feet, fasting and praying for light, for is he not
the greatest light in the woods, in the world? Where are such col-
umns—of sunshine, tangible, accessible, terrestrialized? Well may
I fast, not from bread, but from business, book-making, duty-going,
and other trifles, and great is my reward already for the manly,
treely sacrifice. What giant truths since coming to Gigantea,
what magnificent clusters of Sequoic *becauses*. From here I cannot
recite you one, for you are down a thousand fathoms deep in dark
political quag, not a burr-length less. But I'm in the woods, woods,
woods, and they are in *me-ee-ee*. The King tree and I have sworn
eternal love—sworn it without swearing, and I've taken the sacrament with Douglas squirrel, drunk Sequoia wine, Sequoia blood,
and with its rosy purple drops I am writing this woody gospel
letter.
　I never before knew the virtue of Sequoia juice. Seen with
sunbeams in it, its color is the most royal of all royal purples.
No wonder the Indians instinctively drink it for they know not
what. I wish I were so drunk and Sequoical that I could preach the
green brown woods to all the juiceless world, descending from this
divine wilderness like a John the Baptist, eating Douglas squirrels

and wild honey or wild anything, crying, Repent, for the Kingdom of Sequoia is at hand!

There is balm in these leafy Gileads—pungent burrs and living King juice for all defrauded civilization; for sick grangers and politicians; no need of Salt rivers. Sick or successful, come suck Sequoia and be saved.

Douglas squirrel is so pervaded with rosin and burr juice, his flesh can scarce be eaten even by mountaineers. No wonder he is so charged with magnetism! One of the little lions ran across my feet the other day as I lay resting under a fir, and the effect was a thrill like a battery shock. I would eat him no matter how rosiny for the lightning he holds. I wish I could eat wilder things. Think of the grouse with balsam-scented crop stored with spruce buds, the wild sheep full of glacier meadow grass and daisies azure, and the bear burly and brown as Sequoia, eating pine-burrs and wasps' stings and all; then think of the soft lightningless poultice-like pap reeking upon town tables. No wonder cheeks and legs become flabby and fungoid! I wish I were wilder, and so, bless Sequoia, I will be. There is at least a punky spark in my heart and it may blaze in this autumn gold, fanned by the King. Some of my grandfathers must have been born on a muirland for there is heather in me, and tinctures of bog juices, that send me to Cassiope, and oozing through all my veins impel me unhaltingly through endless glacier meadows, seemingly the deeper and danker the better.

See Sequoia aspiring in the upper skies, every summit modeled in fine cycloidal curves as if pressed into unseen molds, every bole warm in the mellow amber sun. How truly godful in mien! I was talking the other day with a duchess and was struck with the grand bow with which she bade me good-bye and thanked me for the glaciers I gave her, but this forenoon King Sequoia bowed to me down in the grove as I stood gazing, and the highbred gestures of the lady seemed rude by contrast.

There goes Squirrel Douglas, the masterspirit of the treetop. It has just occurred to me how his belly is buffy brown, and his back silver gray. Ever since the first Adam of his race saw trees and burrs, his belly has been rubbing upon buff bark, and his back has been combed with silver needles. Would that some of you, wise—

terribly wise—social scientists, might discover some method of living as true to nature as the buff people of the woods, running as free as the winds and waters among the burrs and filbert thickets of these leafy, mothery woods.

The sun is set, and the star candles are being lighted to show me and Douglas squirrel to bed. Therefore, my Carr, good night. You say, "When are you coming down?" Ask the Lord—Lord Sequoia.

[John Muir]

Yosemite Glaciers

Yosemite Valley, Cal.
September 28.

Two years ago, when picking flowers in the mountains back of Yosemite Valley, I found a book. It was blotted and storm-beaten; all of its outer pages were mealy and crumbly, the paper seeming to dissolve like the snow beneath which it had been buried, but many of the inner pages were well preserved, and though all were more or less stained and torn, whole chapters were easily readable. In just this condition is the great open book of Yosemite glaciers today; its granite pages have been torn and blurred by the same storms that wasted the castaway book. The grand central chapters of the Hoffman, and Tenaya, and Nevada glaciers are stained and corroded by the frosts and rains, yet, nevertheless, they contain scarce one unreadable page; but the outer chapters of the Pohono, and the Illilouette, and the Yosemite Creek, and Ribbon, and Cascade glaciers are all dimmed and eaten away on the bottom, though the tops of their pages have not been so long exposed, and still proclaim in splendid characters the glorious actions of their departed ice. The glacier which filled the basin of Yosemite Creek was the fourth ice stream that flowed to Yosemite Valley. It was about fifteen miles in length by five in breadth at the middle of the main stream, and in many places was not less than one thousand feet in depth. It united with the central glaciers in the valley by a mouth reaching from the east side of El Capitan to Yosemite Point, east of the falls. Its western rim was rayed with short tributaries, and on the north its divide from the Tuolumne glacier was deeply grooved; but few if any of its ridges were here high enough to separate the descending ice into distinct tributaries. The main central trunk flowed nearly south, and, at a distance of about ten miles, separated into three nearly equal branches, which were turned abruptly to the east.

BRANCH BASINS

Those branch basins are laid among the highest spurs of the Hoffman range, and abound in small, bright lakes, set in the solid granite without the usual terminal moraine dam. The structure of those dividing spurs is exactly similar, all three appearing as if ruins of one mountain, or rather as perfect units hewn from one mountain rock during long ages of glacial activity. As their north sides are precipitous, and as they extend east and west, they were enabled to shelter and keep alive their hiding glaciers long after the death of the main trunk. Their basins are still dazzling bright, and their lakes have as yet accumulated but narrow rings of border meadow, because their feeding streams have had but little time to carry the sand of which they are made. The east bank of the main stream, all the way from the three forks to the mouth, is a continuous, regular wall, which also forms the west bank of Indian Canyon glacier basin. The tributaries of the west side of the main basin touched the east tributaries of the cascade, and the great Tuolumne glacier from Mount Dana, the mightiest ice river of this whole region, flowed past on the north. The declivity of the tributaries was great, especially those which flowed from the spurs of the Hoffman on the Tuolumne divide, but the main stream was rather level, and in approaching Yosemite was compelled to make a considerable ascent back of Eagle Cliff. To the concentrated currents of the central glaciers, and to the levelness and width of mouth of this one, we in a great measure owe the present height of the Yosemite Falls. Yosemite Creek lives the most tranquil life of all the large streams that leap into the valley, the others occupying the canyons of narrower and, consequently, of deeper glaciers, while yet far from the valley, abound in loud falls and snowy cascades, but Yosemite Creek flows straight on through smooth meadows and hollows, with only two or three gentle cascades, and now and then a row of soothing, rumbling rapids, biding its time, and hoarding up the best music and poetry of its life for the one anthem at Yosemite, as planned by the ice.

YOSEMITE BASIN

When a bird's-eye view of Yosemite Basin is obtained from any of its upper domes, it is seen to possess a great number of dense patches of black forest, planted in abrupt contact with bare, gray rocks. Those forest plots mark the number and the size of all the entire and fragmentary moraines of the basin, as the later eroding agents have not yet had sufficient time to form a soil fit for the vigorous life of large trees.

Wherever a deep-wombed tributary was laid against a narrow ridge, and was also shielded from the sun by compassing rock shadows, there we invariably find one or more small terminal moraines, because when such tributaries were melted off from the trunk they retired to those upper strongholds of shade, and lived and worked in full independence, and the moraines which they built are left entire because the water-collecting basins behind them are too small to make streams large enough to wash them away; but in the basins of exposed tributaries there are no terminal moraines, because their glaciers died *with* the trunk. Medial and lateral moraines are common upon all the outside slopes, some of them nearly perfect in form; but down in the main basin there is not left one unaltered moraine of any kind, immense floods having washed down and leveled them into border meadows for the present stream, and into sandy flower beds and fields for forests.

GLACIER HISTORY

Such was Yosemite glacier, and such is its basin, the magnificent work of its hands. There is sublimity in the life of a glacier. Water rivers work openly, and so do the rains and the gentle dews, and the great sea also grasping all the world; and even this universal ocean of breath, though invisible, yet speaks aloud in a thousand voices and proclaims its modes of working and its power; but glaciers work apart from men, exerting their tremendous energies in silence and darkness, outspread, spirit-like, brooding above pre-destined rocks unknown to light, unborn, working on unwearied through unmeasured times, unhalting as the stars, until at length, their creations complete, their mountains brought forth, homes made for the meadows and the lakes, moraine banks for chosen flowers, and fields for waiting forests, earnest, calm as when they came in crystals from the sky, they depart.

The great valley itself, together with all of its various domes and walls, was brought forth and fashioned by a grand combi-nation of glaciers, acting in certain directions against granite of peculiar physical structure. All of the rocks and mountains and lakes and meadows of the whole upper Merced basin received their specific forms and carvings almost entirely from this same agency of ice.

I have been drifting about among the rocks of this region for sev-eral years, anxious to spell out some of the mountain truths which are written here; and since the number, and magnitude, and sig-nificance of these ice rivers began to appear, I have become anxious for more exact knowledge regarding them; with this object, sup-plying myself with blankets and bread, I climbed out of Yosemite by Indian Canyon, and am now searching the upper rocks and moraines for readable glacier manuscript.

I meant to begin by exploring the main trunk glacier of Yosemite Creek, together with all of its rim tributaries one by one, gath-ering what data I could find regarding their depth, direction of flow, the kind and amount of work which each had done, etc., but when I was upon the El Capitan Mountain, seeking for the western shore of the main stream, I discovered that the Yosemite Creek glacier was not the lowest ice stream which flowed to the val-ley, but that the Ribbon Stream basin west of El Capitan had also been occupied by a glacier, which flowed nearly south, and united with the main central glaciers of the summits in the valley below El Capitan.

Ribbon Stream Basin

I spent two days in this new basin. It must have been one of the smallest ice streams that entered the valley being only about four miles in length by three in width. It received some small tributaries from the slopes of El Capitan ridge, which flowed south 35° west; but most of its ice was derived from a spur of the Hoffman group, running nearly southwest. The slope of its bed is steep and pretty regular, and it must have flowed with considerable velocity. I have not thus far discovered any of the original striated surfaces, though possibly some patches may still exist somewhere in the basin upon hard plates of quartz, or where a boulder of protecting form has settled upon a rounded surface. I found many such patches in the basin of Yosemite Glacier; one within half a mile of the top of the falls—about two feet square in extent of surface, very perfect in polish, and its striae distinct, although the surrounding unprotected rock is disintegrated to a depth of at least four inches. As this small glacier sloped fully with unsheltered bosom to the sun, it was one of the first to die, and of course its tablets have been longer exposed to blurring rains and dews, and all eroding agents; but notwithstanding the countless blotting, crumbling storms which have fallen upon the historic lithographs of its surface, the great truth of its former existence, printed in characters of moraine and meadow and valley groove, is still as clear as when every one of its pebbles and newborn rocks gleamed forth the full unshadowed poetry of its whole life. With the exception of a few castled piles and broken domes upon its east banks, its basin is rather smooth and lake-like, but it has charming meadows, most interesting in their present flora and glacier history, and noble forests of the two silver firs (*Picea amabilis* and *P. grandis*) planted upon moraines spread out and leveled by overflowing waters.

These researches in the basin of the Ribbon Creek recalled some observations made by me some time ago in the lower portions of the basins of the Cascade and Tamarac streams, and I now thought it probable that careful search would discover abundant traces of glacial action in those basins also. Accordingly, on reaching the highest northern slope of the Ribbon, I obtained comprehensive views of both the Cascade and Tamarac basins, and amid their countless adornments could note many forms of lake and rock which appeared as genuine glacier characters unmarred and unaltered. Running down the bare slope of an icy-looking canyon, in less than half an hour I came upon a large patch of the old glacier bed, polished and striated, with the direction of the flow of the long dead stream clearly written—South 40° West. This proved to be the lowest, easternmost tributary of the Cascade glacier. I proceeded westward as far as the Cascade meadows on the Mono trail, then turning to the right, entered the mouth of the tributary at the head of the meadows. Here there is a well-defined terminal moraine, and the ends of both ridges which formed the banks of the ice are broken and precipitous, giving evidence of great pressure. I followed up this tributary to its source on the west bank of the Yosemite glacier about two miles north of the Mono trail, and throughout its entire length there is abundance of polished tablets with moraines, rock sculpture, etc., giving glacier testimony as clear and indisputable as can be found in the most recent glacier pathways of the Alps.

Vanished Glaciers

I would gladly have explored the main trunk of this beautiful basin, from its highest snows upon the divide of the Tuolumne, to its mouth in the Merced Canyon below Yosemite, but alas! I had not sufficient bread; besides, I felt sure that I should also have to explore the Tamarac basin, and, following westward among the fainter, most changed, and covered glacier pathways, I might probably be called as far as the end of the Pilot Peak Ridge. Therefore, I concluded to leave those lower chapters for future lessons, and go on with the easier Yosemite pages which I had already begun.

But before taking leave of those lower streams let me distinctly state that in my opinion future investigation will discover proofs of the existence in the earlier ages of Sierra Nevada ice, of vast glaciers which flowed to the very foot of the range. Already it is clear that all of the upper basins were filled with ice so deep and universal that but few of the highest crests and ridges were sufficiently great to separate it into individual glaciers, many of the highest mountains having been flowed over and rounded like the boulders in a river. Glaciers poured into Yosemite by every one of its canyons, and at a comparatively recent period of its history, its northern wall, with perhaps the single exception of the crest of Eagle Cliff, was covered by one unbroken flow of ice, the several glaciers having united before they reached the wall.

SEPTEMBER 30—Last evening I was camped in a small round glacier meadow, at the head of the easternmost tributary of the cascade. The meadow was velvet with grass, and circled with the most beautiful of all the conifers, the Williamson spruce. I built a great fire, and the daisies of the sod rayed as if conscious of a sun. As I lay on my back, feeling the presence of the trees—gleaming upon the dark, and gushing with life—coming closer and closer about me, and saw the small round sky coming down with its stars to dome my trees, I said, "Never was mountain mansion more beautiful, more spiritual, never was mortal wanderer more blessedly homed." When the sun rose, my charmed walls were taken down, the trees returned to the common fund of the forest, and my little sky fused back into the measureless blue, I was left upon common ground to follow my glacier labor.

YOSEMITE RIVER BASINS

I followed the main Yosemite River northward, passing round the head of the second Yosemite tributary, which flowed about northeast until bent southward by the main current. About noon, I came to the basin of the third ice tributary of the west rim, a place of domes which had long engaged my attention, and as I was anxious to study their structure, and the various moraines, etc., of the little glacier which had issued from their midst, I camped here close to the foot of two of the most beautiful of the domes, in a sheltered hollow, the womb of the glacier. At the foot of these two domes are two lakes exactly alike in size and history, beautiful as any I ever beheld; first there is the crystal water center, then a yellowish fringe of *Carex*, which has long arching leaves that dip into the water, then a beveled bossy border of yellow *Sphagnum* moss, exactly marking the limits of the lake, farther back is a narrow zone of dryer meadow, smooth and purple with grasses which grow in soft plushy sods, interrupted here and there by clumpy gatherings of blue berry bushes. The purple *Kalmia* grows here also, and the splendidly flowered *Phyllodoce*, but these are small and weave into the sod, spreading low in the grasses and glowing with them. Beside these flowering shrubs, the meadow is lightly sprinkled with daisies and *Dodecatheons* and white violets, most lovely meadows divinely adjusted to most lovely lakes.

In the afternoon I followed down the bed of the tributary to its junction with the main glacier; then, turning to the right, crossed the mouths of the first two tributaries, which I had passed in the morning; then, bearing east, examined a cross section of the main trunk, and reached camp by following up the north bank of the tributary. Between the three tributaries above-mentioned are well defined medial moraines, having been preserved from leveling floods by their position on the higher slopes, with but small water-collecting basins behind them. Down at their junctions, where they were swept round by the main stream, is a large, level field of moraine matter, which, like all the drift fields of this basin, is planted with heavy forests, composed mainly of a pine and fir (*Pinus contorta*, and *Picea amabilis*). This forest is now on fire. I wanted to pass through it, but feared the falling trees. As I stood watching the flapping flames and estimating chances, a tall blazing pine crashed across the gap which I wished to pass, and in a few minutes two more fell. This stirred a broken thought about special providences, and caused me to go around out of danger. *Pinus contorta* is very susceptible of fire, as it grows very close, in grovy thickets, and usually every tree is trickled and beaded with gum. The summit forests are almost entirely composed of this pine.

DEER IN THE VALLEY

Emerging from this wooded moraine I found a great quantity of loose separate boulders upon a polished hilltop, which had formed a part of the bottom of the main ice stream. They were of extraordinary size, some large as houses, and I started northward to seek the mountain from which they had been torn. I had gone but a little way when I discovered a deer quietly feeding upon a narrow strip of green meadow about sixty or seventy yards ahead of me. As the wind blew gently toward it, I thought the opportunity good for testing the truth of hunters' accounts of the deer's wonderful keenness of scent, and stood quite still, and as the deer continued to feed tranquilly, only casting round his head upon his shoulder occasionally to drive away the flies, I began to think that his nose was no better than my own, when suddenly, as if pierced by a bullet, he sprang up into the air and galloped confusedly off without turning to look; but in a few seconds, as if doubtful of the direction of the danger, he came bounding back, caught a glimpse of me, and ran off a second time in a settled direction.

The Yosemite basin is a favorite summer home of the deer. The leguminous vines and juicy grasses of the great moraines supply savory food, while the many high hidings of the Hoffman Mountains, accessible by narrow passes, afford favorite shelter. Grizzly and brown bears also love Yosemite Creek. Berries of the dwarf manzanita, and acorns of the dwarf live oak are abundant upon the dry hilltops; and these with some plants, and the larvae of black ants, are the favorite food of bears, if varied occasionally by a stolen sheep or a shepherd. The gorges of the Tuolumne Canyon, on the north end of the basin, are their principal hiding places in this region. Higher in the range their food is not plentiful, and lower they are molested by man.

On returning to camp I passed three of the domes of the north bank, and was struck with the exact similarity of their structure, the same concentric layers, with a perpendicular cleavage also, but less perfectly developed and more irregular. This little dome tributary, about two-and-a-half miles long by one-and-a-half wide, must have been one of the most beautiful of the basin; all of its upper circling rim is adorned with domes, some half born, sunk in the parent rock; some broken and torn upon the sides by the ice, and a few nearly perfect, from their greater strength of structure or more favorable position. The two lakes above described are the only ones of the tributary basin, both domes and lakes handiwork of the glacier.

A Glacier's Death

In the waning days of this mountain ice, when the main river began to shallow and break like a summer cloud, its crests and domes rising higher and higher, and island rocks coming to light far out in the main current, then many a tributary died, and this one, cut off from its trunk, moved slowly back amid the gurgling and gushing of its bleeding rills, until, crouching in the shadows of this half-mile hollow, it lived a feeble separate life. Here its days come and go, and the hiding glacier lives and works. It brings boulders and sand and fine dust polishings from its sheltering domes and canyons, building up a terminal moraine, which forms a dam for the waters which issue from it; and beneath, working in the dark, it scoops a shallow lake basin. Again the glacier retires, crouching under cooler shadows, and a cluster of steady years enables the dying glacier to make yet another moraine dam like the first; and, where the granite begins to rise in curves to form the upper dam, it scoops another lake. Its last work is done, and it dies. The twin lakes are full of pure green water, and floating masses of snow and broken ice. The domes, perfect in sculpture, gleam in newborn purity, lakes and domes reflecting each other bright as the ice which made them. God's seasons circle on, glad brooks born of the snow and the rain sing in the rocks, and carry sand to the naked lakes, and, in the fullness of time comes many a chosen plant; first a lowly *Carex* with dark brown spikes, then taller sedges and rushes, fixing a shallow soil, and now come many grasses, and daisies, and blooming shrubs, until lake and meadow growing throughout the season like a flower in summer, develop to the perfect beauty of today.

How softly comes night to the mountains. Shadows grow upon all the landscape; only the Hoffman Peaks are open to the sun. Down in this hollow it is twilight, and my two domes, more impressive than in broad day, seem to approach me. They are not vast and over-spiritual, like Yosemite Tissiack, but comprehensible and companionable, and susceptible of human affinities. The darkness grows, and all of their finer sculpture dims. Now the great arches and deep curves sink also, and the whole structure is massed in black against the starry sky.

I have set fire to two pine logs, and the neighboring trees are coming to my charmed circle of light. The two-leaved pine, with sprays and tassels innumerable, the silver fir, with magnificent frouded whorls of shining boughs, and the graceful nodding spruce, dripping with cones, and seeming yet more spiritual in this campfire light. Grandly do my logs give back their light, slow gleaned from suns of a hundred summers, garnered beautifully away in dotted cells and in beads of amber gum; and, together with this outgush of light, seems to flow all the other riches of their life, and their living companions are looking down as if to witness their perfect and beautiful death. But I am weary and must rest. Good night to my two logs and two lakes, and to my two domes high and black on the sky, with a cluster of stars between.

Indian Tribes in the Yosemite Valley

In the wild gold years of 1849 and '50, the Indian tribes along the western Sierra foothills became alarmed at the sudden invasion of their acorn orchard and game fields by miners, and soon began to make war upon them, in their usual murdering, plundering style. This continued until the United States Indian Commissioners succeeded in gathering them into reservations, some peacefully, others by burning their villages and stores of food. The Yosemite or Grizzly Bear tribe, fancying themselves secure in their deep mountain stronghold, were the most troublesome and defiant of all, and it was while the Mariposa battalion, under command of Major Savage, was trying to capture this warlike tribe and conduct them to the Fresno reservation that their deep mountain home, the Yosemite Valley, was discovered. From a camp on the south fork of the Merced, Major Savage sent Indian runners to the bands who were supposed to be hiding in the mountains, instructing them to tell the Indians that if they would come in and make treaty with the Commissioners they would be furnished with food and clothing and be protected, but if they did not come in he would make war upon them and kill them all. None of the Yosemite Indians responded to this general message, but when a special messenger was sent to the chief he appeared the next day.

He came entirely alone and stood in dignified silence before one of the guards until invited to enter the camp. He was recognized by one of the friendly Indians as Tenaya, the old chief of the Grizzlies, and, after they had been supplied with food, Major Savage, with the aid of Indian interpreters, informed him of the wishes of the Commissioners. But the old chief was very suspicious of Savage and feared that he was taking this method of getting the tribe into his power for the purpose of revenging his personal wrong. Savage told him if he would go to the Commissioners and make peace with them as the other tribes had done there would be no more war. Tenaya inquired what was the object of taking all the Indians to the San Joaquin plain. "My people," said he, "do not want anything from the Great Father you tell me about. The Great Spirit is our father and he has always supplied us with all we need. We do not want anything from white men. Our women are able to do our work. Go, then. Let us remain in the mountains where we were born, where the ashes of our fathers have been given to the wind. I have said enough."

To this the Major answered abruptly in Indian style: "If you and your people have all you desire, why do you steal our horses and mules? Why do you rob the miners' camps? Why do you murder the white men and plunder and burn their houses?"

Tenaya was silent for some time. He evidently understood what the Major had said, for he replied, "My young men have sometimes taken horses and mules from the whites. This was wrong. It is not wrong to take the property of enemies who have wronged my people. My young men believed that the gold diggers were our enemies. We now know they are not and we shall be glad to live in peace with them. We will stay here and be friends. My people do not want to go to the plains. Some of the tribes who have gone there are very bad. We cannot live with them. Here we can defend ourselves."

To this the Major Savage firmly said, "Your people must go to the Commissioners. If they do not your young men will again steal horses and kill and plunder the whites. It was your people who robbed my stores, burned my houses and murdered my men. It they do not make a treaty, your whole tribe will be destroyed. Not one of them will be left alive."

To this the old chief replied, "It is useless to talk to you about who destroyed your property and killed your people. I am old and you can kill me if you will, but it is useless to lie to you who know more than all the Indians. Therefore I will not lie to you but if you will let me return to my people I will bring them in." He was allowed to go. The next day he came back and said his people were on the way to our camp to go with the men sent by the Great Father, who was so good and rich.

Another day passed but no Indians from the deep Valley appeared. The old chief said that the snow was so deep and his village was so far down that it took a long time to climb out of it. After waiting still another day the expedition started for the Valley. When Tenaya was questioned as to the route and distance he said that the snow was so deep that the horses could not go through it. Old Tenaya was taken along as guide. When the party had gone about half-way to the Valley they met the Yosemites on their way to the camp on the south fork. There were only seventy-two of them and when the old chief was asked what had become of the rest of his band, he replied, "This is all of my people that are willing to go with me to the plains. All the rest have gone with their wives and children over the mountains to the Mono and Tuolumne tribes." Savage told Tenaya that he was not telling the truth, for Indians could not cross the mountains in the deep snow, and that he knew they must still be at his village or hiding somewhere near it. The tribe had been estimated to number over two hundred. Major Savage then said to him, "You may return to camp with your people and I will take one of your young men with me to your village to see your people who will not come. They will come if I find them." "You will not find any of my people there," said Tenaya; "I do not know where they are. My tribe is small. Many of the people of my tribe have come from other tribes and if they go to the plains and are seen they will be killed by the friends of those with whom they have quarreled. I was told that I was growing old and it was well that I should go, but that young and strong men can find plenty in the mountains: therefore, why should they go to the hot plains to be penned up like horses and cattle? My heart has been sore since that talk but I am now willing to go, for it is best for my people."

PART FOUR:

The Global Adventurer

Eskimos and Walrus

STEAMER CORWIN, PLOVER BAY, JUNE 15, 1881.

We left our anchorage in St. Lawrence Bay at four in the morning, June 7, and steered once more for Plover Bay. The norther that had been blowing so long gave place to a light southerly breeze, and a gentle dusting of snow was falling. In the afternoon the sea became smooth and glassy as a mountain lake, and the clouds lifted, gradually unveiling the Siberian coast up to the tops of the mountains. First the black bluffs, standing close to the water, came in sight; then the white slopes, and then one summit after another until a continuous range forty or fifty miles long could be seen from one point of view, forming a very beautiful landscape. Smooth, dull, dark water in the foreground; next, a broad belt of ice mostly white like snow, with numerous masses of blue and black shade among its jagged, uplifted blocks. Then a strip of comparatively low shore, black and gray; and back of that the pure white mountains, with only here and there dark spots, where the rock faces are too steep for snow to lie upon. Sharp peaks were seen, fluted by avalanches; glacier wombs, delicate in curve and outline as shells; rounded, overswept brows and domes, and long, withdrawing valleys leading back into the highest alpine groups, whence flowed noble glaciers in imposing ranks into what is now Bering Sea.

We had hoped the gale had broken and driven away the floe that barred our way on the fifth [of June], but while yet thirty miles from the entrance of the bay we were again stopped by an immense field of heavy ice that stretched from the shore southeastward as far as the eye could reach. We pushed slowly into the edge of it a few miles, looking for some opening, but the man in the crow's nest reported it all solid ahead and no water in sight. We thereupon steamed out and steered across to St. Lawrence Island to bide our time.

While sailing amid the loose blocks of ice that form the edge of the pack, we saw a walrus, and soon afterward a second one with its young. The captain shot and killed the mother from the pilot-house, and the dinghy was lowered to tow it alongside. The eyes of our Indian passengers sparkled with delight in expectation of good meat after enduring poor fare aboard the ship. After floating for eight or ten minutes, she sank to the bottom and was lost—a sad fate and a luckless deed.

It was pitiful to see the young one swimming around its dying mother, heeding neither the ship nor the boat. They are said to be very affectionate and bold in the defense of one another against every enemy whatever. We have as yet seen but few, though in some places they are found in countless thousands. Many vessels are exclusively employed in killing them on the eastern Greenland coast, and along some portions of the coast of Asia. Here also, the whalers, when they have poor success in whaling, devote themselves to walrus hunting, both for the oil they yield and for the valuable ivory. The latter is worth from forty to seventy cents per pound in San Francisco, and a pair of large tusks weighs from eight to ten pounds.

Along all the coasts, both of Asia and of America, the natives hunt and kill this animal, which to them is hardly less important for food and other uses than the seals. A large walrus is said to weigh from one to two tons. Its tough hide is used for cordage, and to cover canoes. The flesh is excellent, while the ivory formerly was employed for spear heads and other uses, and is now an important article of trade for guns, ammunition, calico, bread, flour, molasses, etc. The natives now kill a good many whales, having obtained lances and harpoons from the whites. Bone, in good years, is more important than the ivory, and furs are traded, also, in considerable quantity. By all these means they obtain more of the white man's goods than is well used. They probably were better off before they were possessed of a single civilized blessing—so many are the evils accompanying them!

Our Chukchi passenger does not appear to entertain a very good opinion of the St. Lawrence natives. He advised the captain to keep a close watch of those he allowed to come aboard. We asked him today the Chukchi name of ice, which he gave as "eigleegle." When we said that another of his people called it "tingting," he replied that that was the way poor common people spoke the word, but that rich people, the upper aristocratic class to which he belonged, called it "eigleegle." His father, being a rich man, had three wives; most of his tribe, he said, have only one.

At nine o'clock in the evening we were still more than an hour's run from St. Lawrence Island, though according to reckoning we should have reached the northeast end of the island at eight o'clock. We had been carried north about sixteen miles, since leaving St. Lawrence Bay, by the current setting through the strait. The water, having been driven south by the north gale, was pouring north with greater velocity than ordinary. The sky was a mass of dark, grainless cloud, banded slightly near the northwest horizon; one band, a degree in breadth above the sun, was deep indigo, with a few short streaks of orange and red. We have not seen a star since leaving San Francisco, and have seen the sun perfectly cloudless only once! We came to anchor near the northwest end of the island about midnight.

The next day, the eighth of June, was calm and mild. A canoe with ten men and women came alongside this morning, just arrived from Plover Bay, on their way home. They made signs of weariness, having pulled hard against this heavy current. The distance is fifty miles. It is not easy to understand how they manage to find their way in thick weather, when it is difficult enough for seamen with charts and compass.

In trying to account for the observed similarity between the peoples of the opposite shores of Asia and America, and the faunas and floras, scientists have long been combating a difficulty that does not exist save in their own minds. They have suggested that canoes and ships from both shores either were wrecked and drifted from one to the other, or that natives crossed on the ice which every year fills Bering Strait. As today, so from time immemorial canoes have crossed for trade or mere pleasure, steering by the swell of the sea when out of sight of land. As to crossing on the ice, the natives tell me that they frequently go with their dogsleds from the Siberian side to the Diomedes, those halfway houses along the route, but seldom or never from the Diomedes to the American side, on account of the movements of the ice. But, though both means of communication, assumed to account for distribution as it is found to exist today, were left out, land communication in any case undoubtedly existed, just previous to the glacial period, as far south as the Aleutian Islands, and northward beyond the mouth of the strait.

While groping in the dense fogs that hang over this region, sailors find their way at times by the flight of the innumerable seabirds that come and go from the sea to the shore. The direction, at least, of the land is indicated, which is very important in the case of small islands. How the birds find their way is a mystery.

This canoe alongside was "two sleeps" in making the passage. Time, I suppose, is reckoned by sleeps during summer, as there is no night and only one day. They at once began to trade eagerly, seeming to fear that they would be left unvisited, now that the whalers have all gone to the Arctic. In the forenoon, after the natives had left, we took advantage of the calm weather to go in search of the wrecked *Lolita*, which went ashore last fall a few miles to the north of here. On the way we passed through a good deal of ice in flat cakes that had been formed in a deep still bay, sheltered from floating ice which jams and packs it. This ice did not seem to be more than two or three feet thick, possibly the depth to which it froze last winter less the amount melted and evaporated since spring commenced.

Walruses, in groups numbering from two to fifty, were lying on cakes of ice. They were too shy, however, to be approached within shooting range, though many attempts were made. Some of the animals were as bulky, apparently, as oxen. They would awaken at the sound of the vessel crunching through the loose ice, lift their heads and rear as high as possible, then drop or plunge into the water. The ponderous fellows took headers in large groups; twenty pairs of flippers sometimes were in the air at once. They can stay under water five or six minutes, then come up to blow. If they are near the ship they dive again instantly, going down like porpoises, always exposing a large curving mass of their body while dropping their heads, and, lastly, their flippers are stretched aloft for an instant. Sometimes they show fight, make combined attacks on boats, and defend one another bravely. The cakes on which they congregate are of course very dirty, and show to a great distance. Since they soon sink when killed in the water, they are hunted mostly on the ice, and, when it is rough and hummocky, are easily approached.

We were not successful in finding the *Lolita*, so we steamed back to our anchorage in the lee of a high bluff near the Eskimo village. Soon three or four canoes came alongside, loaded with furs, ivory, and whalebone. Molasses, which they carry away in bladders and seal skins, is with them a favorite article of trade. Mixed with flour and blocks of "black skin," it is esteemed, by Eskimo palates, a dish fit for the gods. A group of listeners laughed heartily when I described a mixture that I thought would be to their taste. They smacked their lips, and shouted, "Yes! Yes!" One brought as a present to our Chukchi, the reindeer man's son, a chunk of "black skin" that, in color and odor, seemed to be more than a year old. He, no doubt, judged that our Chukchi, if not starving, was at least faring poorly on civilized trash.

A study of the different Eskimo faces, while important trades were pending, was very interesting. They are better behaved than white men, not half so greedy, shameless, or dishonest. I made a few sketches of marked faces. One, who received a fathom of calico more than was agreed upon, seemed extravagantly delighted and grateful. He was lost in admiration of the captain, whose hand he shook heartily.

We continued at anchor here the following day, June 9. It was snowing and the decks were sloppy. Several canoe loads of Eskimos came aboard, and there was a brisk trade in furs, mostly reindeer hides and parkas for winter use; also fox [skins] and some whalebone and walrus ivory. Flour and molasses were the articles most in demand. Some of the women, heedless of the weather, brought their boys, girls, and babies. One little thing that the proud mother held up for our admiration smiled delightfully, exposing her two precious new teeth. No happier baby could be found in warm parlors, where loving attendants anticipate every want and the looms of the world afford their best in the way of soft fabrics. She looked gaily out at the strange colors about her from her bit of a fur bag, and when she fell asleep, her mother laid her upon three oars that were set side by side across the canoe. The snowflakes fell on her face, yet she slept soundly for hours while I watched her, and she never cried. All the youngsters had to be furnished with a little bread which both fathers and mothers begged for them, saying, "He *little* fellow, *little* fellow."

Four walrus heads were brought aboard and the ivory sold, while the natives, men and women, sat down to dine on them with butcher knives. They cut off the flesh and ate it raw, apparently with good relish. As usual, each mouthful was cut off while held between the teeth. To our surprise they never cut themselves. They seemed to enjoy selecting tidbits from different parts of the head, turning it over frequently and examining pieces here and there, like a family leisurely finishing the wrecked hull of a last day's dinner turkey.

These people interest me greatly, and it is worth coming far to know them, however slightly. The smile, or, rather, broad grin of that Eskimo baby went directly to my heart, and I shall remember it as long as I live. When its features had subsided into perfect repose, the laugh gone from its dark eyes, and the lips closed over its two teeth, I could make its sweet smile bloom out again as often as I nodded and chirruped to it. Heaven bless it! Some of the boys, too, lads from eight to twelve years of age, were well behaved, bashful, and usually laughed and turned away their faces when looked at. But there was a response in their eyes which made you feel that they are your very brothers.

Stickeen vs. the Glacier

Stickeen seemed able for anything. Doubtless we could have weathered the storm for one night, dancing on a flat spot to keep from freezing, and I faced the threat without feeling anything like despair; but we were hungry and wet, and the wind from the mountains was still thick with snow and bitterly cold, so of course that night would have seemed a very long one. I could not see far enough through the blurring snow to judge in which general direction the least dangerous route lay, while the few dim, momentary glimpses I caught of mountains through rifts in the flying clouds were far from encouraging either as weather signs or as guides. I had simply to grope my way from crevasse to crevasse, holding a general direction by the ice structure, which was not to be seen everywhere, and partly by the wind. Again and again I was put to my mettle, but Stickeen followed easily, his nerve apparently growing more unflinching as the danger increased. So it always is with mountaineers when hard beset. Running hard and jumping, holding every minute of the remaining daylight, poor as it was, precious, we doggedly persevered and tried to hope that every difficult crevasse we overcame would prove to be the last of its kind. But on the contrary, as we advanced they became more deadly trying.

At length our way was barred by a very wide and straight crevasse, which I traced rapidly northward a mile or so without finding a crossing or hope of one; then down the glacier about as far, to where it united with another uncrossable crevasse. In all this distance of perhaps two miles there was only one place where I could possibly jump it, but the width of this jump was the utmost I dared attempt, while the danger of slipping on the farther side was so great that I was loath to try it. Furthermore, the side I was on was about a foot higher than the other, and even with this advantage the crevasse seemed dangerously wide. One is liable to underestimate the width of crevasses where the magnitudes in general are great. I therefore stared at this one mighty keenly, estimating its width and the shape of the edge on the farther side, until I thought that I could jump it if necessary, but that in case I should be compelled to jump back from the lower side I might fail. Now, a cautious mountaineer seldom takes a step on unknown ground which seems at all dangerous that he cannot retrace in case he should be stopped by unseen obstacles ahead. This is the rule of mountaineers who live long, and, though in haste, I compelled myself to sit down and calmly deliberate before I broke it.

Retracing my devious path in imagination as if it were drawn on a chart, I saw that I was recrossing the glacier a mile or two farther upstream than the course pursued in the morning, and that I was now entangled in a section I had not before seen. Should I risk this dangerous jump, or try to regain the woods on the west shore, make a fire, and have only hunger to endure while waiting for a new day? I had already crossed so broad a stretch of dangerous ice that I saw it would be difficult to get back to the woods through the storm before dark, and the attempt would most likely result in a dismal night-dance on the glacier; while just beyond the present barrier the surface seemed more promising, and the east shore was now perhaps about as near as the west. I was therefore eager to go on. But this wide jump was a dreadful obstacle.

At length, because of the dangers already behind me, I determined to venture against those that might be ahead, jumped and landed well, but with so little to spare that I more than ever dreaded being compelled to take that jump back from the lower side. Stickeen followed, making nothing of it, and we ran eagerly forward, hoping we were leaving all our troubles behind. But within the distance of a few hundred yards we were stopped by the widest crevasse yet encountered. Of course I made haste to explore it, hoping all might yet be remedied by finding a bridge or a way around either end. About three-fourths of a mile upstream I found that it united with the one we had just crossed, as I feared it would. Then, tracing it down, I found it joined the same crevasse at the lower end also, maintaining throughout its whole course a width of forty to fifty feet. Thus to my dismay I discovered that we were on a narrow island about two miles long, with two barely possible ways of escape: one back by the way we came, the other ahead by an almost inaccessible sliver-bridge that crossed the great crevasse from near the middle of it!

After this nerve-trying discovery I ran back to the sliver-bridge and cautiously examined it. Crevasses, caused by strains from variations in the rate of motion of different parts of the glacier and convexities in the channel, are mere cracks when they first open, so narrow as hardly to admit the blade of a pocketknife, and gradually widen according to the extent of the strain and the depth of the glacier. Now some of these cracks are interrupted, like the cracks in wood, and in opening, the strip of ice between overlapping ends is dragged out and may maintain a continuous connection between the sides, just as the two sides of a slivered crack in wood that is being split are connected. Some crevasses remain open for months or even years, and by the melting of their sides continue to increase in width long after the opening strain has ceased; while the sliver-bridges, level on top at first and perfectly safe, are at length melted to thin, vertical, knife-edged blades, the upper portion being most exposed to the weather; and since the exposure is greatest in the middle, they at length curve downward like the cables of suspension bridges. This one was evidently very old, for it had been weathered and wasted until it was the most dangerous and inaccessible that ever lay in my way. The width of the crevasse was here about fifty feet, and the sliver crossing diagonally was about seventy feet long; its thin knife-edge near the middle was depressed twenty-five or thirty feet below the level of the glacier, and the upcurving ends were attached to the sides eight or ten feet below the brink. Getting down the nearly vertical wall to the end of the sliver and up the other side were the main difficulties, and they seemed all but insurmountable. Of the many perils encountered in my years of wandering on mountains and glaciers none seemed so plain and stern and merciless as this. And it was presented when we were wet to the skin and hungry, the sky dark with quick driving snow, and the night near. But we were forced to face it. It was a tremendous necessity.

Beginning, not immediately above the sunken end of the bridge, but a little to one side, I cut a deep hollow on the brink for my knees to rest in. Then, leaning over, with my short-handled ax, I cut a step sixteen or eighteen inches below, which on account of the sheerness of the wall was necessarily shallow. That step, however, was well made; its floor sloped slightly inward and formed a good hold for my heels. Then, slipping cautiously upon it, and crouching as low as possible, with my left side toward the wall I steadied myself against the wind with my left hand in a slight notch, while with the right I cut other similar steps and notches in succession, guarding against losing balance by glinting of the ax, or by wind gusts, for life and death were in every stroke and in the niceness of finish of every foothold.

After the end of the bridge was reached I chipped it down until I had made a level platform six or eight inches wide, and it was a trying thing to poise on this little slippery platform while bending over to get safely astride of the sliver. Crossing was then comparatively easy by chipping off the sharp edge with short, careful strokes, and hitching forward an inch or two at a time, keeping my balance with my knees pressed against the sides. The tremendous abyss on either hand I studiously ignored. To me the edge of that blue sliver was then all the world. But the most trying part of the adventure, after working my way across inch by inch and chipping another small platform, was to rise from the safe position astride and to cut a stepladder in the nearly vertical face of the wall— chipping, climbing, holding on with feet and fingers in mere notches. At such times one's whole body is eye, and common skill and fortitude are replaced by power beyond our call or knowledge. Never before had I been so long under deadly strain. How I got up that cliff I could never tell. The thing seemed to have been done by somebody else. I never have held death in contempt, though in the course of my explorations I have oftentimes felt that to meet one's fate on a noble mountain, or in the heart of a glacier, would be blessed as compared with death from disease, or from some shabby lowland accident. But the best death, quick and crystal-pure, set so glaringly open before us, is hard enough to face, even though we feel gratefully sure that we have already had happiness enough for a dozen lives.

But poor Stickeen, the wee, hairy, sleekit beastie, think of him! When I had decided to dare the bridge, and while I was on my knees chipping a hollow on the rounded brow above it, he came behind me, pushed his head past my shoulder, looked down and across, scanned the sliver and its approaches with his mysterious eyes, then looked me in the face with a startled air of surprise and concern, and began to mutter and whine, saying as plainly as if speaking with words, "Surely, you are not going into that awful place." This was the first time I had seen him gaze deliberately into a crevasse, or into my face with an eager, speaking, troubled look. That he should have recognized and appreciated the danger at the first glance showed wonderful sagacity. Never before had the daring midget seemed to know that ice was slippery or that there was any such thing as danger anywhere. His looks and tones of voice when he began to complain and speak his fears were so human that I unconsciously talked to him in sympathy as I would to a frightened boy, and in trying to calm his fears perhaps in some measure moderated my own. "Hush your fears, my boy," I said, "we will get across safe, though it is not going to be easy. No right way is easy in this rough world. We must risk our lives to save them. At the worst we can only slip, and then how grand a grave we will have, and by and by our nice bones will do good in the terminal moraine."

But my sermon was far from reassuring him: he began to cry, and after taking another piercing look at the tremendous gulf, ran away in desperate excitement, seeking some other crossing. By the time he got back, baffled of course, I had made a step or two. I dared not look back, but he made himself heard, and when he saw that I was certainly bent on crossing he cried aloud in despair. The danger was enough to daunt anybody, but it seems wonderful that he should have been able to weigh and appreciate it so justly. No mountaineer could have seen it more quickly or judged it more wisely, discriminating between real and apparent peril.

When I gained the other side, he screamed louder than ever, and after running back and forth in vain search for a way of escape, he would return to the brink of the crevasse above the bridge, moaning and wailing as if in the bitterness of death. Could this be the silent, philosophic Stickeen? I shouted encouragement, telling him the bridge was not as bad as it looked, that I had left it flat and safe for his feet, and he could walk it easily. But he was afraid to try. Strange so small an animal should be capable of such big, wise fears. I called again and again in a reassuring tone to come on and fear nothing; that he could come if he would only try. He would hush for a moment, look down again at the bridge, and shout his unshakable conviction that he could never, never come that way; then lie back in despair, as if howling, "O-o-oh! What a place! No-o-o, I can never go-o-o down there!" His natural composure and courage had vanished utterly in a tumultuous storm of fear. Had the danger been less, his distress would have seemed ridiculous. But in this dismal, merciless abyss lay the shadow of death, and his heartrending cries might well have called Heaven to his help. Perhaps they did. So hidden before, he was now transparent, and one could see the workings of his heart and mind like the movements of a clock out of its case. His voice and gestures, hopes and fears, were so perfectly human that none could mistake them, while he seemed to understand every word of mine. I was troubled at the thought of having to leave him out all night, and of the danger of not finding him in the morning. It seemed impossible to get him to venture. To compel him to try through fear of being abandoned, I started off as if leaving him to his fate, and disappeared back of a hummock, but this did no good; he only lay down and moaned in utter hopeless misery. So, after hiding a few minutes, I went back to the brink of the crevasse, and in a severe tone of voice shouted across to him that now I must certainly leave him, I could wait no longer, and that, if he would not come, all I could promise was that I would return to seek him next day. I warned him that if he went back to the woods the wolves would kill him, and finished by urging him once more by words and gestures to come on, come on.

He knew very well what I meant, and at last, with the courage of despair, hushed and breathless, he crouched down on the brink in the hollow I had made for my knees, pressed his body against the ice as if trying to get the advantage of the friction of every hair, gazed into the first step, put his little feet together and slid them slowly, slowly over the edge and down into it, bunching all four in it and almost standing on his head. Then, without lifting his feet, as well as I could see through the snow, he slowly worked them over the edge of the step and down into the next and the next in succession in the same way, and gained the end of the bridge. Then, lifting his feet with the regularity and slowness of the vibrations of a seconds pendulum, as if counting and measuring *one-two-three*, holding himself steady against the gusty wind, and giving separate attention to each little step, he gained the foot of the cliff, while I was on my knees leaning over to give him a lift should he succeed in getting within reach of my arm. Here he halted in dead silence, and it was here I feared he might fail, for dogs are poor climbers. I had no cord. If I had had one, I would have dropped a noose over his head and hauled him up. But while I was thinking whether an available cord might be made out of clothing, he was looking keenly into the series of notched steps and finger-holds I had made, as if counting them, and fixing the position of each one of them in his mind. Then suddenly up he came in a springy rush, hooking his paws into the steps and notches so quickly that I could not see how it was done, and whizzed past my head, safe at last!

And now came a scene! "Well done, well done, little boy! Brave boy!" I cried, trying to catch and caress him, but he would not be caught. Never before or since have I seen anything like so passionate a revulsion from the depths of despair to exultant, triumphant, uncontrollable joy. He flashed and darted hither and thither as if fairly demented, screaming and shouting, swirling round and round in giddy loops and circles like a leaf in a whirlwind; lying down, and rolling over and over, sidewise and heels over head, and pouring forth a tumultuous flood of hysterical cries and sobs and gasping mutterings. When I ran up to him to shake him, fearing he might die of joy, he flashed off two or three hundred yards, his feet in a mist of motion; then, turning suddenly, came back in a wild rush and launched himself at my face, almost knocking me down, all the time screeching and screaming and shouting as if saying, "Saved! saved! saved!" Then away again, dropping suddenly at times with his feet in the air, trembling and fairly sobbing. Such passionate emotion was enough to kill him. Moses' stately song of triumph after escaping the Egyptians and the Red Sea was nothing to it. Who could have guessed the capacity of the dull, enduring little fellow for all that most stirs this mortal frame? Nobody could have helped crying with him!

But there is nothing like work for toning down excessive fear or joy. So I ran ahead, calling him in as gruff a voice as I could command to come on and stop his nonsense, for we had far to go and it would soon be dark.

Voyage to East Africa

JANUARY 16.

Fine weather. Left for Victoria Falls about 12:30 p.m. Fine ride along sand flat at base of mountains, gradually rising. At 5:15 at Worsuster. Beautiful town, in long beautiful, level, boulder-strewn glacier valley, in some places several miles wide, perhaps a hundred miles long or more. Finely sculptured mountain range on both sides. Water rather scarce, small streams. Like valleys in S. California. Small vineyards here and there. Grapes ripe. Grain harvested.

At the head of this long mountain-walled valley, our heavy train of a dozen coaches, drawn and pushed by two powerful engines, climbed on wonderful grades (7 or 8%) and curves out upon a vast plateau like those of Arizona in flora bounded by level-topped buttes and peaks. Saw small black monkey walking slowly and indignantly away from the passing train near the head of the pass. Not a cloud in the sky until near sundown when beautiful crimson horizontal plumes decorated the lower sky all around. A most glorious day in every way. The stars shone bright as we sped on over the apparently boundless plain.

JANUARY 17.

Glorious sunrise. Cloudless. All day on great plateau. Soil red and tawny. Ant nest, dome-shaped, narrow, eighteen inches high. Saw man on horseback driving a flock of ostriches. A remarkable sight to me. Crossed only one river by a fine steel bridge. The Orange River, I suppose. Arrived at Kimberly about 7:20 p.m. Marvelous city, of enormous gray dumps of material hoisted from the diamond beds. Left Kimberly and the diamond pits at 8:30 p.m. Dry desert, seemingly endless.

JANUARY 18.
Wonderful change. All the broad plain or plateau green and even flowery here and there, and dotted with bushes and small trees. Mimosa, etc. Some of them in flower. Gradually increasing in size and number until they darkened the landscape in the distance like forests. Only a few rounding hills or low mountains visible in the vast expanse. At 10:00 a.m. ran suddenly into a region of rounded glaciated hills of metamorphic slate out of which we emerged in about an hour to a wide plain, green and flowery with dark forested mountains in the distance. Ground near the track densely covered with bushes, mostly with yellow-green foliage. Here the first trees were found, twenty to thirty feet high, eighteen inches in diameter, with lavish undergrowth of bushes. This plain, with its low forest, extends with great regularity for one hundred and fifty miles or more. The train had been running through it at twenty miles speed over six and a half hours, and now, at sundown, there is no sign of reaching the limit of this strange forest and plain, a smooth sandstone plain, apparently boundless. Only a small group of peaks to the westward, seen about 6:00 p.m. A red sandstone in rounded moutonnée masses and ridgy pavements show here and there through the almost continuous tufted sod of grasses like Buffalo grass.

JANUARY 19.
Cloudy and cool. Magnificent sunrise. Huge compound wing-shaped masses of clouds, changing to deep velvety maroon and magenta. A truly glorious spectacle. The same nearly level plateau. Green, lightly forested, stretching on and on with no boundary in sight save the sky. No mountains visible. A sea of verdure. Arrived Bulwayo about 7:00 a.m. Scrawny breakfast at station. Walked through the town. Forest becoming more varied. Tall palms common, and the low, pale green dwarf species. The ground hillocky.

JANUARY 20.

Arrive at Victoria Falls station at 7:00 a.m. and have enjoyed a wonderful day, wonderful in many ways; one of the greatest of the great tree days of my lucky life. Inquiring at the hotel if there were any baobabs in the neighborhood, the manager said that he had never heard of a baobab. I explained that it was a large tree, one of the largest of the great trees of the world, and that I had heard that some of them grew at no great distance from here.

After many anxious inquiries I found a bright Negro boy guide who led me direct to the long-dreamed-of African *Adansonia digitata*. I found a large number at a distance of only about a mile or a mile and a half from the head of the Falls, and not over half a mile back from the bank of the river. I discovered specimens showing their different forms, varying from twelve to twenty-four feet in diameter. Most of them about seventy-five to ninety feet high and very wide-spreading, the main branches large, often four to six feet in diameter, gradually dividing into comparatively slender branchlets; many of them drooping, and well-clad with rather pale green five to seven or even nine-fingered leaves. I found a few of the fruits that had fallen on the ground and also some of the wilted flowers. The flowers are white, circular, and about six inches in diameter. This grand tree was first discovered by Michael Adanson of the West Coast near Sierra Leone. It also extends considerably to the north at the head of the Senegal River. I afterwards found it in great abundance at Mozambique, Zanzibar, Desersalaan, Panga, and Mombasa on the East Coast. A red-flowered species *A. madagascariensis* is found on the island of that name. A third species has been found in Australia, *A. gregorii*. It is often called monkey-bread tree. Also cream of tartar tree, from the pleasantly acid juice of the fruit furnishing a refreshing drink. This wonderful tree belongs to the malvaceae. The timber is so soft and spongy that it has no merchantable use, though I was informed that large rain-water tanks were sometimes dug in the broad body of the living tree. It grows scattered here and there among other trees in the general forest, and is easily recognized by its remarkably smooth skin-like bark, and its massive trunk and branches. Altogether I measured and sketched about a dozen specimens. The fruit is green, about six inches long and three in diameter, hanging straight down, and very conspicuous. The leaves are thin, delicate, and smooth. About three to four or five inches long and wide. The bark is gray in color, wonderfully smooth, shining, wrinkled here and there, and slightly corrugated horizontally, but with no furrow like the bark of most other trees. It looks like leather, or the skin of the hippopotamus. On my return trip I noticed a good many in the woods from the car window seventy miles or more to the southward of the falls. On the return trip to Bulwayo I enjoyed the company of Captain Murray, who has charge of the mounted police through a large part of Rhodesia north and south from the Victoria Falls. He kindly promised to send me photographs of the most telling of the Rhodesian trees. Took me to his headquarters at Bulwayo and arranged for my journey to Beira.

JANUARY 21.
Arrived Bulwayo at 7:00 this morning, having left the Falls at 12:20 p.m. yesterday. Enjoyed view of part of the forest that I had passed through at night on my way North. The baobab is the most interesting feature of the forest for seventy miles south of Victoria Falls. Went to Grand Hotel, Bulwayo. The town is spread over a large level area. The buildings sparsely sprinkled. Will take long to form continuous streets. At hotel all day, resting after wild baobab and Zambesi joy. Strange tree. In bark like skin of elephant. Corrugated and wrinkled like skin of hippopotamus. Very smooth and glossy. Gray, whitish some places. Beautiful five to seven-parted leaves. Huge limbs but well clothed with leaves. So striking in size and form it is easily recognized at a distance of several miles.

The Falls too are grand and novel, and are already drawing large numbers of tourists from all parts of the world. Smoke-like spray is ever ascending, watering the woods in the neighborhood with constant drizzling showers. Large area near the Falls called the "Rainy Woods."

Among the other notable trees of the baobab forest is the Mopani, a fine, large leguminous tree with hard, valuable wood. The Maruba, another large tree, the fruit of which is edible. *Erythima tomentosa*, something like the baobab at a distance, also leguminous. Kigelia has fruit shaped like sausage two feet in length. This large tree is also seen at Victoria Falls. Common in equatorial Africa. It has a sturdy trunk with rough furrowed bark like an oak. Purple tulip-like blossoms. Also three species of palms.

FEBRUARY 7.
Start at noon for Antebbe, Uganda. Heavy rain in the morning. Baobabs common along the railroad for twenty or thirty miles, but smaller as the coast is left, though the soil is good. Why is this? Hills grassy, trees and shrubs scattered, fire-scourged. Glacier features. Mountains blue in the distance. Had good fortune as usual in finding two pleasant traveling companions, one a Swiss, who kindly shared his fine luncheon with me, as there is no dining car on the train. At night he gave me one of his rugs as there was no bedding on the train. This friend is a professional hunter with headquarters at Nairobi. The other is Arch-Deacon Binns. Two others joined us in our compartment in the middle of the night. Scotch. One who had often been in Dunbar and knew my friends there. Heard him pronounce "John" and knew him for a Scotchman in the dark, though I was half asleep.

FEBRUARY 8.
Country more and more distinctly glacial. See hundreds or thousands of hartbeests and other antelopes, some within stone's throw of the track. Large number of wild ostriches. Grassy plains. No trees or shrubs for miles and miles. Great hills and mountains in the distance. Lovely country. Glacial drift common. Arrived Nairobi at 11:15 a.m. Went to Norfolk Hotel.

FEBRUARY 9.
At Hotel. Fine scenery. Heavy rain. Great need of increased hotel accommodations. In rare weather conditions Kaillimanjara visible

one hundred and fifty miles distant from here. Rained for three days on most of way from Mombasa. Rainy season usually begins in March in this part of British East Africa.

FEBRUARY 10.
Left Nairobi for Port Florence at noon. Rainy until after dark. Never saw rain so early in the season in the last fourteen years, though only about a month earlier than usual. Railroad runs through beautiful mountain scenery, patches of forest with open grassy prairies, filled-up lake basins. Views of large main valley, very broad, fine in its main lines. Tawny in color from dry grass. Juniper common. Used for lumber, but splits too freely for some purposes, and as usual all the older trees are eaten with dry rot in the center. This is true of all the many species of juniper. Grand views of the great valley. Was kindly given a blanket and pillow by Mr. Rees, the night being very cold, although almost directly on the equator. The elevation at the highest point the railroad passed over during the night was about 8,000 feet above sea level.

FEBRUARY 11.
Arrived at Port Florence about 7:00 a.m. Went aboard the good little steamer *Clement Hill* and started for Antebbe at 10:00 a.m. Wonderful picturesque scenery. Low, green, half-forested hills with mountains in the distance. Not very high. Some perhaps about 6,000 feet above the sea. The Victoria Nyanza one of the largest in the world. Second in size only to Lake Superior. Hippopotamus common around the muddy and reedy shores. The lake is comparatively shallow, only about 240 feet at the deepest part. Anchored at dark.

FEBRUARY 12.
Started at daybreak. Arrived at Antebbe about 11:00 a.m. at head of a beautiful bay. Measured one tree about six feet in diameter a little way back from the shore. Many are three or four feet, with fine, wide-spreading head. One tree, of moderate size, had noble digitate leaves, fourteen or more, eighteen inches wide. Petioles two feet long. Mr. Rees took me to the Uganda Protectorate.
    Spathodia nilotica, has very large flowers.

Canarium schweinfurthii, very large tree.
Thevetia nerriforia, red.
Bauhinia triandra, double leaf.
Randia dummetorium.
Solianum macaranthum.
Maesopsis berchemoides.
Pipledenia africana.
Monodora myristica.

Mr. Rees took me to the Botanical Gardens. Saw the Manager, who kindly ordered his head gardener to show me over the garden and give me specimens of all I wished. A bright, scholarly fellow, Singalese, from Ceylon. There is a species of mourning dove hereabouts which says "Too hot for anything." A lovely creeper going up straight on smooth-barked tree in regular zigzags.

FEBRUARY 13.
Started for Kompali at daylight. Arrived about 9:00 a.m. Ride in jinrikisha from port to village, a distance of about seven miles, through beautiful landscape. Extensive and thrifty banana orchards. The fruit red instead of yellow. Interesting swamps full of the famous papyrus growing here naturally. Charming red, blue and white water lilies in the harbor in glorious abundance. Arrived at Kompali in an hour and a half. Returned in one hour. My jinrikisha was hauled and pushed by three lusty Negroes, two pushing and the other in the shafts. Chanted all the way while trotting, the leader rapidly improvising a line, and the chorus sounded like "Harry Trunk! Harry Trunk!" The leader would say: "The white man is going to see our pretty town." "Harry Trunk. Harry Trunk." "He sees the black man's fine banana field." "Harry Trunk. Harry Trunk." "He is looking at the birds in the trees." "Harry Trunk. Harry Trunk." "The white man's far from his cold, cold home." "Harry Trunk. Harry Trunk." Etc.

FEBRUARY 14.
Started for Jinja at 5:00 a.m. Arrived at 11:30 a.m. From the village I went to see the Ripon Falls at the outlet of the great lake, the main

head fountain of the Nile, the distance from the port being only a little over a mile. The fall is only about fifteen or twenty feet over a bar of resisting rock. The fall is divided into three parts and makes a magnificent show of foam. Large numbers of alligators were sunning themselves on the farther bank at the head of the falls, while fishes in large numbers are constantly springing in wide curves in their attempts to ascend the cascade to enter the lake. The broad stream setting out in rapids on its 3,330 mile course is very impressive.

"In 1852 Sir Roderick Murchison advanced the hypothesis that Africa south of the Sahara Desert was a continent of great antiquity, and simplicity, which had maintained the form of a great basin ever since the age of the new red sandstone. He based his theory on the work of Bain, the pioneer of South African geology, summarized in a paper entitled 'On the Antiquity of the Physical Geography of Inner Africa' by R. Murchison, in which he claims that the country is of interest because it was geologically unique in the long conservation of ancient terrestrial conditions."

The famous Ngrurunga (water holes) from J. W. Gregory's book entitled *The Great Rift Valley*.

FEBRUARY 15.
Start for Port Florence at 4:00 a.m. Arrived at 5:00 p.m.

FEBRUARY 16.
Got aboard the train on the return journey to Mombasa at 7:30 a.m. From the Port a long level valley six to eight miles wide looks like a filled-in part of the Port Florence arm of the lake, extending twenty or thirty miles to the southward, bounded on the west by a range of bold bluffs, separated by wide cirques here and there; and on the east by smooth terraces, extending lakeward parallel to the bluffs. Native villages and fields along the valley. Water lilies at Port Florence, and papyrus. *Kigelia* trees in fruit here and magnificent figs. One near Port Florence, green with dark green foliage, had fruit a half inch in diameter. The trunk about eight feet in diameter, with a dense dome-shaped broad head something like the great banyan of India. Wild mountains after leaving the lake plains,

through which the railroad has been built at great cost. Twenty or thirty steel trestles over gorgeous and fluting ravines in close succession. Some of the passengers saw a lion by the roadside.

FEBRUARY 17.

Very cold night. Slept cold, with heavy underclothing, coat and vest, overcoat, and a thick blanket. Elevation of the region about 6,000 to 8,000 feet above the sea. Colder than the Tuolumne Meadows in the spring, though 3,000 feet higher than here. Passed through dense forests about noon, but the greater part of the way is through grassy hills with only detached patches of brush and trees. Extensive wheat fields here and there. Yesterday afternoon and this forenoon near Nivahsa Station and Lake. This remarkable lake is surrounded by a picturesque mountain and hills. Water said to be fresh, though without any visible outlet. Between Nivasha and Nairoba saw Mt. Kilimanjara and Kenia, and many antelopes and zebra, all within short distances of the railroad, and remarkably tame. The latter most at ease as the train rolled past. This afternoon soon after leaving Nairoba saw hundreds or thousands of antelopes, two droves of zebras, and a few ostriches. Some of the antelopes were lying down within a stone's throw of the track, a few of which lay still. Others rose and gazed at the train, and a few ran off to a distance of a quarter of a mile or so. These fine beasts were on a beautiful treeless shrubless plain or prairie. After coming to a plain dotted with small trees and bushes none of the animals were seen. Some parts of the prairie were roughened with moraine boulders, and some places weathered from the bedrock, which occurs here and there in large patches without any kind of soil, something like glacier pavements, with potholes here and there, weathered out by the rain and wind. Some beds of quartz pebbles with large boulders here and there. The stream channels very shallow. All signs point to glaciation no great geological time ago. Most of the animals seen today were on the Athi plain, and have learned that the nearer the railroad the safer they are from the attack of either men or lions. A strip along the track a mile in width had been reserved as a game refuge, which the animals have been quick to discover and flock into it, from all the adjacent region. Saw Kilimanjara again this afternoon. Only its broad base was visible. The head and main body cloud mantled. Saw also many baobabs two hundred and fifty miles or more from Mombasa. One stood near the Makinda Station within six feet or so from the railroad track.

Part Five:

The Planet Steward

God's First Temples: How Shall We Preserve Our Forests?

RECORD-UNION:

The forests of coniferous trees growing on our mountain ranges are by far the most destructible of the natural resources of California. Our gold, and silver, and cinnabar are stored in the rocks, locked up in the safest of all banks, so that notwithstanding the world has been making a run upon them for the last twenty-five years, they still pay out steadily and will probably continue to do so centuries hence, like rivers pouring from perennial mountain fountains. The riches of our magnificent soil beds are also comparatively safe, because even the most barbarous methods of wildcat farming cannot effect complete destruction, and however great the impoverishment produced, full restoration of fertility is always possible to the enlightened farmer. But our forest belts are being burned and cut down and wasted like a field of unprotected grain, and once destroyed can never be wholly restored, even by centuries of persistent and painstaking cultivation.

The practical importance of the preservation of our forests is augmented by their relations to climate, soil, and streams. Strip off the woods with their underbrush from the mountain flanks, and the whole state, the lowlands as well as the highlands, would gradually change into a desert. During rainfalls, and when the winter snow was melting, every stream would become a destructive torrent, overflowing its banks, stripping off and carrying away the fertile soils, filling up the lower river channels, and overspreading the lowland fields with detritus to a vastly more destructive degree than all the washings from hydraulic mines concerning which we now hear so much. Dripping forests give rise to moist sheets and currents of air, and the sod of grasses and underbrush thus fostered, together with the roots of trees themselves, absorb and hold back rains and melting snow, yet allowing them to ooze and percolate and flow gently in useful fertilizing streams. Indeed every pine needle and rootlet, as well as fallen trunks and large clasping roots, may be regarded as dams, hoarding the bounty of storm clouds and dispensing it as blessings all through the summer, instead of allowing it to gather and rush headlong in short-lived, devastating floods. Streams taking their rise in deep woods flow unfailingly as those derived from the eternal ice and snow of the Alps. So constant, indeed, and apparent is the relationship between forests and never-failing springs, that effect is frequently mistaken for cause, it being often asserted that line forests will grow only along streamsides where their roots are well watered, when in fact the forests themselves produce many of the streams flowing through them.

The main forest belt of the Sierra is restricted to the western flank, and extends unbrokenly from one end of the range to the other at an elevation of from three to eight thousand feet above sea level. The great master-existence of these noble woods is *Sequoia gigantea*, or big tree. Only two species of sequoia are known to exist in the world. Both belong to California, one being found only in the Sierra, the other (*Sequoia sempervirens*) in the Coast Ranges, although no less than five distinct fossil species have been discovered in the tertiary and cretaceous rocks of Greenland. I would like to call attention to this noble tree, with special reference to its preservation. The species extends from the well known Calaveras groves on the north, to the head of Deer Creek on the south, near the big bend of the Kern River, a distance of about two hundred miles, at an elevation above sea level of from about five to eight thousand feet. From the Calaveras to the south fork of King's River, it occurs only in small isolated groves, and so sparsely and irregularly distributed that two gaps occur nearly forty miles in width, the one between the Calaveras and Tuolumne groves, the other between those of the Fresno and King's rivers. From King's River the belt extends across the broad, rugged basins of the Kaweah and Tule rivers to its southern boundary on Deer Creek, interrupted only by deep, rocky canyons, the width of this portion of the belt being from three to ten miles.

In the northern groves few young trees or saplings are found ready to take the places of the failing old ones, and because these ancient, childless sequoias are the only ones known to botanists, the species has been generally regarded as doomed to speedy extinction, as being nothing more than an expiring remnant of an ancient flora, and that therefore there is no use trying to save it or to prolong its few dying days. This, however, is in the main a mistaken notion, for the Sierra as it now exists never had an ancient flora. All the species now growing on the range have been planted since the close of the glacial period, and the Big Tree has never formed a greater part of these postglacial forests than it does today, however widely it may have been distributed throughout preglacial forests.

In tracing the belt southward, all the phenomena bearing upon its history goes to show that the dominion of *Sequoia gigantea*, as king of California trees, is not yet passing away. No tree in the woods seems more firmly established, or more safely settled in accordance with climate and soil. They fill the woods and form the principal tree, growing heartily on solid ledges, along water courses, in the deep, moist soil of meadows, and upon avalanche and glacial debris, with a multitude of thrifty seedlings and saplings crowding around the aged, ready to take their places and rule the woods.

Nevertheless, Nature in her grandly deliberate way keeps up a rotation of forest crops. Species develop and die like individuals, animal as well as plant. Man himself will as surely become extinct as sequoia or mastodon, and be at length known only as a fossil. Changes of this kind are, however, exceedingly slow in their movements, and, as far as the lives of individuals are concerned, such changes have no appreciable effect. Sequoia seems scarcely further past prime as a species than its companion firs (*Picea amabilis* and *P. grandis*), and judging from its present condition and its ancient history, as far as I have been able to decipher it, our sequoia will live and flourish gloriously until A.D. 15,000 at least—probably for longer—that is, if it be allowed to remain in the hands of nature.

But waste and pure destruction are already taking place at a terrible rate, and unless protective measures be speedily invented and enforced, in a few years this noblest tree-species in the world will present only a few hacked and scarred remnants. The great enemies of forests are fire and the ax. The destructive effects of these, as compared with those caused by the operations of nature, are instantaneous. Floods undermine and kill many a tree, storm winds bend and break, landslips and avalanches overwhelm whole groves, lightning shatters and burns, but the combined effects of all these amount only to a wholesome beauty-producing culture. Last summer I found some five sawmills located in or near the lower edge of the sequoia belt, all of which saw more or less of the big tree into lumber. One of these (Hyde's), situated on the north fork of the Kaweah, cut no less than two million feet of sequoia lumber last season. Most of the Fresno big trees are doomed to feed the mills recently erected near them, and a company has been formed by Chas. Converse to cut the noble forest on the south fork of King's River. In these milling operations, waste far exceeds use. After the choice young manageable trees have been felled, the woods are cleared of limbs and refuse by burning, and in these clearing fires, made with reference to further operations, all the young seedlings and saplings are destroyed, together with many valuable fallen trees and old trees, too large to be cut, thus effectually cutting off all hopes of a renewal of the forest.

These ravages, however, of mill-fires and mill-axes are small as compared with those of the "sheep men's" fires. Incredible numbers of sheep are driven to the mountain pastures every summer, and in order to make easy paths and to improve the pastures, running fires are set everywhere to burn off the old logs and underbrush. These fires are far more universal and destructive than would be guessed. They sweep through nearly the entire forest belt of the range from one extremity to the other, and in the dry weather, before the coming on of winter storms, are very destructive to all kinds of young trees, and especially to sequoia, whose loose, fibrous bark catches and burns at once. Excepting the Calaveras, I, last summer, examined every sequoia grove in the range, together with the main belt extending across the basins of Kaweah and Tule, and found everywhere the most deplorable waste from this cause. Indians burn off underbrush to facilitate deer hunting. Campers of all kinds often permit fires to run, so also do mill-men, but the fires of sheep men probably form more than 90 percent of all destructive fires that sweep the woods.

Fire, then, is the arch destroyer of our forests, and sequoia forests suffer most of all. The young trees are most easily fire killed; the old are most easily burned, and the prostrate trunks, which never rot and would remain valuable until our tenth centennial, are reduced to ashes.

In European countries, especially in France, Germany, Italy, and Austria, the economies of forestry have been carefully studied under the auspices of government, with the most beneficial results. Whether our loose-jointed government is really able or willing to do anything in the matter remains to be seen. If our lawmakers were to discover and enforce any method tending to lessen even in a small degree the destruction going on, they would thus cover a multitude of legislative sins in the eyes of every tree lover. I am satisfied, however, that the question can be intelligently discussed only after a careful survey of our forests has been made, together with studies of the forces now acting upon them.

A law was constructed some years ago making the cutting down of sequoias over sixteen feet in diameter illegal. A more absurd and shortsighted piece of legislation could not be conceived. All the young trees might be cut and burned, and all the old ones might be burned but not cut.

Sacramento Daily Record-Union
February 5, 1876

The Wild Parks and Forest Reservations of the West

Keep not standing fix'd and rooted,
　Briskly venture, briskly roam;
Head and hand, where'er thou foot it,
　And stout heart are still at home.
In each land the sun does visit
　We are gay, whate'er betide:
To give room for wandering is it
　That the world was made so wide.

The tendency nowadays to wander in wildernesses is delightful to see. Thousands of tired, nerve-shaken, over-civilized people are beginning to find out that going to the mountains is going home; that wildness is a necessity; and that mountain parks and reservations are useful not only as fountains of timber and irrigating rivers, but as fountains of life. Awakening from the stupefying effects of the vice of over-industry and the deadly apathy of luxury, they are trying as best they can to mix and enrich their own little ongoings with those of nature, and to get rid of rust and disease. Briskly venturing and roaming, some are washing off sins and cobweb cares of the devil's spinning in all-day storms on mountains; sauntering in rosiny pine woods or in gentian meadows, brushing through chaparral, bending down and parting sweet, flowery sprays; tracing rivers to their sources, getting in touch with the nerves of Mother Earth; jumping from rock to rock, feeling the life of them, learning the songs of them, panting in whole-souled exercise, and rejoicing in deep, long-drawn breaths of pure wildness. This is fine and natural and full of promise. So also is the growing interest in the care and preservation of forests and wild places in general, and in the half-wild parks and gardens of towns. Even the scenery habit in its most artificial forms, mixed with spectacles, silliness, and kodaks; its devotees arrayed more gorgeously than scarlet tanagers, frightening the wild game with red umbrellas—even this is encouraging, and may well be regarded as a hopeful sign of the times.

All the western mountains are still rich in wildness, and by means of good roads are being brought nearer civilization every year. To the sane and free it will hardly seem necessary to cross the continent in search of wild beauty, however easy the way, for they find it in abundance wherever they chance to be. Like Thoreau they see forests in orchards and patches of huckleberry brush, and oceans in ponds and drops of dew. Few in these hot, dim, strenuous times are quite sane or free; choked with care like clocks full of dust, laboriously doing so much good and making so much money—or so little—they are no longer good for themselves.

When, like a merchant taking a list of his goods, we take stock of our wildness, we are glad to see how much of even the most destructible kind is still unspoiled. Looking at our continent as scenery when it was all wild, lying between beautiful seas, the starry sky above it, the starry rocks beneath it, to compare its sides, the East and the West, would be like comparing the sides of a rainbow. But it is no longer equally beautiful. The rainbows of today are, I suppose, as bright as those that first spanned the sky; and some of our landscapes are growing more beautiful from year to year, notwithstanding the clearing, trampling work of civilization. New plants and animals are enriching woods and gardens, and many landscapes wholly new, with divine sculpture and architecture, are just now coming to the light of day as the mantling folds of creative glaciers are being withdrawn, and life in a thousand cheerful, beautiful forms is pushing into them, and newborn rivers are beginning to sing and shine in them. The old rivers, too, are growing longer, like healthy trees, gaining new branches and lakes as the residual glaciers at their highest sources on the mountains recede, while the root-like branches in their flat deltas are at the same time spreading farther and wider into the seas and making new lands.

Under the control of the vast mysterious forces of the interior of the earth, all the continents and islands are slowly rising or sinking. Most of the mountains are diminishing in size under the wearing action of the weather, though a few are increasing in height and girth, especially the volcanic ones, as fresh floods of molten rocks are piled on their summits and spread in successive layers, like the wood-rings of trees, on their sides. New mountains, also, are being created from time to time as islands in lakes and seas, or as subordinate cones on the slopes of old ones, thus in some measure balancing the waste of old beauty with new. Man, too, is making many far-reaching changes. This most influential half animal, half angel is rapidly multiplying and spreading, covering the seas and lakes with ships, the land with huts, hotels, cathedrals, and clustered city shops and homes, so that soon, it would seem, we may have to go farther than Nansen to find a good sound solitude. None of nature's landscapes are ugly so long as they are wild; and much, we can say comfortingly, must always be in great part wild, particularly the sea and the sky, the floods of light from the stars, and the warm, unspoilable heart of the earth, infinitely beautiful, though only dimly visible to the eye of imagination. The geysers, too, spouting from the hot underworld; the steady, long-lasting glaciers on the mountains, obedient only to the sun; Yosemite domes and the tremendous grandeur of rocky canyons and mountains in general—these must always be wild, for man can change them and mar them hardly more than can the butterflies that hover above them. But the continent's outer beauty is fast passing away, especially the plant part of it, the most destructible and most universally charming of all.

Only thirty years ago, the great Central Valley of California, five hundred miles long and fifty miles wide, was one bed of golden and purple flowers. Now it is ploughed and pastured out of existence, gone forever—scarce a memory of it left in fence corners and along the bluffs of the streams. The gardens of the Sierra, also, and the noble forests in both the reserved and unreserved portions are sadly hacked and trampled, notwithstanding the ruggedness of the topography—all excepting those of the parks guarded by a few soldiers. In the noblest forests of the world, the ground, once divinely beautiful, is desolate and repulsive, like a face ravaged by disease. This is true also of many other Pacific Coast and Rocky Mountain valleys and forests. The same fate, sooner or later, is awaiting them all, unless awakening public opinion comes forward to stop it. Even the great deserts in Arizona, Nevada, Utah, and New Mexico, which offer so little to attract settlers, and which a few years ago pioneers were afraid of, as places of desolation and death, are now taken as pastures at the rate of one or two square miles per cow, and of course their plant treasures are passing away—the delicate *Abronias, Phloxes, Gilias*, etc. Only a few of the bitter, thorny, unbitable shrubs are left, and the sturdy cacti that defend themselves with bayonets and spears.

Most of the wild plant wealth of the East also has vanished— gone into dusty history. Only vestiges of its glorious prairie and woodland wealth remain to bless humanity in boggy, rocky, unploughable places. Fortunately, some of these are purely wild and go far to keep nature's love visible. White water lilies, with rootstocks deep and safe in mud, still send up every summer a Milky Way of starry, fragrant flowers around a thousand lakes, and many a tuft of wild grass waves its panicles on mossy rocks, beyond reach of trampling feet, in company with saxifrages, bluebells, and ferns. Even in the midst of farmers' fields, precious *Sphagnum* bogs, too soft for the feet of cattle, are preserved with their charming plants unchanged—*Chiogenes, Andromeda, Kalmia, Linnaea, Arethusa*, etc. *Calypso borealis* still hides in the arbor vitae swamps of Canada, and away to the southward there are a few unspoiled swamps, big ones, where miasma, snakes, and alligators, like guardian angels, defend their treasures and keep them as pure as paradise. And beside a' that and a' that, the East is blessed with good winters and blossoming clouds that shed white flowers over all the land, covering every scar and making the saddest landscape divine at least once a year.

The most extensive, least spoiled, and most unspoilable of the gardens of the continent are the vast tundras of Alaska. In sum- mer they extend smooth, even, undulating, continuous beds of flowers and leaves from about latitude 62 to the shores of the Arctic Ocean; and in winter sheets of snow flowers make all the country shine, one mass of white radiance like a star. Nor are these Arctic plant people the pitiful frost-pinched unfortunates they are guessed to be by those who have never seen them. Though lowly in stature, keeping near the frozen ground as if loving it, they are bright and cheery, and speak nature's love as plainly as their big relatives of the South. Tenderly happed and tucked in beneath downy snow to sleep through the long, white winter, they make haste to bloom in the spring without trying to grow tall, though some rise high enough to ripple and wave in the wind, and display masses of color—yellow, purple, and blue—so rich that they look like beds of rainbows, and are visible miles and miles away.

As early as June one may find the showy *Geum glaciale* in flower, and the dwarf willows putting forth myriad fuzzy catkins, to be followed quickly, especially on the dryer ground, by *Mertensia, Eritrichium, Polemonium, Oxytropis, Astragalus, Lathyrus, Lupinus, Myosotis, Dodecatheon, Arnica, Chrysanthemum, Nardosmia, Saussurea, Senecio, Erigeron, Matrecaria, Caltha, Valeriana, Stellaria, Tofieldia, Polygonum, Papaver, Phlox, Lychnis, Cheiranthus, Linnaea,* and a host of *Drabas, Saxifrages,* and heathworts, with bright stars and bells in glorious profusion, particularly *Cassiope, Andromeda, Ledum, Pyrola,* and *Vaccinium—Cassiope* the most abundant and beautiful of them all. Many grasses also grow here, and wave fine purple spikes and panicles over the other flowers—*Poa, Aira, Calamagrostis, Alopecurus, Trisetum, Elymus, Festuca, Glyceria,* etc. Even ferns are found thus far north, carefully and comfortably unrolling their precious fronds—*Aspidium, Cystopteris,* and *Woodsia,* all growing on a sumptuous bed of mosses and lichens; not the scaly lichens seen on rails and trees and fallen logs to the southward, but massive, round-headed, finely colored plants like corals, wonderfully beautiful, worth going round the world to see. I should like to mention all the plant friends I found in a summer's wanderings in this cool reserve, but I fear few would care to read their names, although everybody, I am sure, would love them could they see them blooming and rejoicing at home.

On my last visit to the region about Kotzebue Sound, near the middle of September 1881, the weather was so fine and mellow that it suggested the Indian summer of the eastern states. The winds were hushed, the tundra glowed in creamy golden sunshine, and the colors of the ripe foliage of the heathworts, willows, and birch—red, purple, and yellow, in pure bright tones—were enriched with those of berries which were scattered everywhere, as if they had been showered from the clouds like hail. When I was back a mile or two from the shore, reveling in this color-glory, and thinking how fine it would be could I cut a square of the tundra sod of conventional picture size, frame it, and hang it among the paintings on my study walls at home, saying to myself, "Such a nature painting taken at random from any part of the thousand-mile bog would make the other pictures look dim and coarse," I heard merry shouting, and, looking round, saw a band of Eskimos—men, women, and children, loose and hairy like wild animals—running toward me. I could not guess at first what they were seeking, for they seldom leave the shore; but soon they told me, as they threw themselves down, sprawling and laughing, on the mellow bog, and began to feast on the berries. A lively picture they made, and a pleasant one, as they frightened the whirring ptarmigans, and surprised their oily stomachs with the beautiful acid berries of many kinds, and filled sealskin bags with them to carry away for festive days in winter.

Nowhere else on my travels have I seen so much warm-blooded, rejoicing life as in this grand Arctic reservation, by so many regarded as desolate. Not only are there whales in abundance along the shores, and innumerable seals, walruses, and white bears, but on the tundras, great herds of fat reindeer and wild sheep, foxes, hares, mice, piping marmots, and birds. Perhaps more birds are born here than in any other region of equal extent on the continent. Not only do strong-winged hawks, eagles, and waterfowl, to whom the length of the continent is merely a pleasant excursion, come up here every summer in great numbers, but also many short-winged warblers, thrushes, and finches, repairing hither to rear their young in safety, reinforce the plant bloom with their plumage, and sweeten the wilderness with song; flying all the way, some of them, from Florida, Mexico, and Central America. In coming north they are coming home, for they were born here, and they go south only to spend the winter months, as New Englanders go to Florida. Sweet-voiced troubadours, they sing in orange groves and vine-clad magnolia woods in winter, in thickets of dwarf birch and alder in summer, and sing and chatter more or less all the way back and forth, keeping the whole country glad. Oftentimes, in New England, just as the last snow patches are melting and the sap in the maples begins to flow, the blessed wanderers may be heard about orchards and the edges of fields where they have stopped to glean a scanty meal, not tarrying long, knowing they have far to go. Tracing the footsteps of spring, they arrive in their tundra homes in June or July, and set out on their return journey in September, or as soon as their families are able to fly well.

This is nature's own reservation, and every lover of wildness will rejoice with me that by kindly frost it is so well defended. The discovery lately made that it is sprinkled with gold may cause some alarm; for the strangely exciting stuff makes the timid bold enough for anything, and the lazy destructively industrious. Thousands at least half insane are now pushing their way into it, some by the southern passes over the mountains, perchance the first mountains they have ever seen—sprawling, struggling, gasping for breath, as, laden with awkward, merciless burdens of provisions and tools, they climb over rough-angled boulders and cross thin miry bogs. Some are going by the mountains and rivers to the eastward through Canada, tracing the old romantic ways of the Hudson Bay traders; others by Bering Sea and the Yukon, sailing all the way, getting glimpses perhaps of the famous fur seals, the ice floes, and the innumerable islands and bars of the great Alaska river. In spite of frowning hardships and the frozen ground, the Klondike gold will increase the crusading crowds for years to come, but comparatively little harm will be done. Holes will be burned and dug into the hard ground here and there, and into the quartz-ribbed mountains and hills; ragged towns like beaver and muskrat villages will be built, and mills and locomotives will make rumbling, screeching, disenchanting noises; but the miner's pick will not be followed far by the plough, at least not until nature is ready to unlock the frozen soil beds with her slow-turning climate key. On the other hand, the roads of the pioneer miners will lead many a lover of wildness into the heart of the reserve, who without them would never see it.

In the meantime, the wildest health and pleasure grounds accessible and available to tourists seeking escape from care and dust and early death are the parks and reservations of the West. There are four National Parks—the Yellowstone, Yosemite, General Grant, and Sequoia—all within easy reach, and thirty forest reservations, a magnificent realm of woods, most of which, by railroads and trails and open ridges, is also fairly accessible, not only to the determined traveler rejoicing in difficulties, but to those (may their tribe increase) who, not tired, not sick, just naturally take wing every summer in search of wildness. The forty million acres of these reserves are in the main unspoiled as yet, though sadly wasted and threatened on their more open margins by the ax and fire of the lumberman and prospector, and by hoofed locusts, which, like the winged ones, devour every leaf within reach, while the shepherds and owners set fires with the intention of making a blade of grass grow in the place of every tree, but with the result of killing both the grass and the trees.

Thoughts upon National Parks

UNDATED ENTRY; CA. 1895
Yosemite Park is a place of rest, a refuge from the roar and dust and weary, nervous, wasting work of the lowlands, in which one gains the advantages of both solitude and society. Nowhere will you find more company of a soothing peace-be-still kind. Your animal fellow beings, so seldom regarded in civilization, and every rock-brow and mountain, stream, and lake, and every plant soon come to be regarded as brothers; even one learns to like the storms and clouds and tireless winds. This one noble park is big enough and rich enough for a whole life of study and aesthetic enjoyment.

Government protection should be thrown around every wild grove and forest on the mountains, as it is around every private orchard, and the trees in public parks. To say nothing of their value as fountains of timber, they are worth infinitely more than all the gardens and parks of towns.

We believe our forests under rational management will yield a perennial supply of timber for every right use without further diminishing their area, and what is left now of the forest lands which after being surveyed is found to be unfit for agriculture should immediately be withdrawn from private entry and kept for the good of the people for all time. Nearly all our forests in the West are on mountains and cover and protect the fountains of the rivers. They are being more and more deeply invaded and, of course, fires are multiplied; five to ten times as much lumber is burned as is used, to say nothing of the waste of lowlands by destructive floods. As sheep advance, flowers, vegetation, grass, soil, plenty, and poetry vanish. [. . .]

Instead of bands of sheep one may meet new bands of bright girls and boys threading the forest aisles, stepping briskly along, the health and exhilaration of the mountains in every eye. In the exciting times of gold-digging scenery was unnoticed. Many old Californians even, living within a day or two's journey of Yosemite, never saw it; but now in the springtime children go to the park with enthusiasm as if called by the blast of a trumpet.

The park is the poor man's refuge. Few are altogether blind and deaf to the sweet looks and voices of nature. Everybody at heart loves God's beauty because God made everybody.

Sources

Part One: The Visionary Inventor

"Knowledge and Inventions" and "The World and the University" from *The Story of My Boyhood and Youth* (Chs. 7 and 8) from *John Muir: Nature Writings*, William Cronon, ed. (New York: Library of America, 1997), 117–42.

Part Two: The Wandering Minstrel

"Kentucky Forests and Caves and Through the Cumberland Mountains" and "The River Country of Georgia, Through Florida's Swamps and Forests, and across Florida to Cedar Keys," from *A Thousand-Mile Walk to the Gulf* by John Muir (Boston: Houghton Mifflin—Mariner Books, 1916), 9–14; 30–33; 60–63; 103–7; 121–34.

Part Three: The Nature Scribe and Rhapsode

"In Camp on the North Fork of the Merced" and "The Mono Indians of Bloody Cañon" from *My First Summer in the Sierra* (Chs. 2 and 9) by John Muir (Boston, New York: Houghton Mifflin, 1911), 71–79, 214–31.

"A Near View of the High Sierra" and "A Windstorm in the Forest," from *The Mountains of California* (Chs. 4 and 10) by John Muir (Berkeley: Ten Speed Press, Facsimile Edition, 1894, 1977), 48–73; 244–57.

"Yosemite Falls at Midnight," letter from John Muir to Jeanne (Mrs. Ezra S.) Carr, April 3, 1871, from *The Life and Letters of*

John Muir, William Frederic Bade, ed. (Boston: Houghton Mifflin, 1924), 1:249–52.

"Nut Time in Squirrelville," letter from John Muir to Jeanne (Mrs. Ezra S.) Carr, dated "Nut Time," ca. 1870, from *The Life and Letters of John Muir*, 1:270–73.

"Yosemite Glaciers," originally published in the *New York Tribune*, Dec. 5, 1871, from *John Muir: Nature Writings* (New York: Library of America), 577–86.

"A Yosemite Earthquake" and "Indian Tribes of the Yosemite Valley," from *The Yosemite* by John Muir (New York: Doubleday / Anchor Books, 1912, 1962), 59–65; 173–76.

Part Four: The Global Adventurer

"Eskimos and Walrus," from *The Cruise of the Corwin* by John Muir (San Francisco: Sierra Club Books, 1993), 48–55.

"Stickeen vs. the Glacier," from *Stickeen* by John Muir (Berkeley: Heyday Books, 1990), 39–64.

"Voyage to East Africa," from *John Muir's Last Journey*, Michael P. Branch, ed. (Washington, D.C.: Island Press, 2001), 107–14. Reproduced by permission of Island Press, Washington, DC.

Part Five: The Planet Steward

"God's First Temples: How Shall We Preserve Our Forests?" originally published in the *Sacramento Daily Record-Union*, Feb. 5, 1876, from *John Muir: Nature Writings* (New York: Library of America), 629–33.

"The Wild Parks and Forest Reservations of the West," originally published in the *Atlantic Monthly*, August 1897, from *Our National Parks* by John Muir (San Francisco: Sierra Club Books, 1991), 1–10.

"Thoughts upon National Parks" (ca. 1895), from *John of the Mountains: The Unpublished Journals of John Muir*, ed. Linnie Marsh Wolfe, reprint edition (Madison: University of Wisconsin Press, 1938, 1979), 350–54. Reproduced by permission of John Muir Papers, Holt-Atherton Special Collections, University of The Pacific Library. © 1984 Muir-Hanna Trust.

Major Works by John Muir
(in order of publication)

The Mountains of California (1894)
Our National Parks (1901)
Stickeen (1909)
My First Summer in the Sierra (1911)
The Yosemite (1912)
The Story of My Boyhood and Youth (1913)
Travels in Alaska (1915)
A Thousand-Mile Walk to the Gulf (1916)

About the Editor

Fred D. White, a native Californian, was born in Los Angeles in 1943, in the very same hospital—California Hospital—in which John Muir had died twenty-nine years earlier. White received his Ph.D. in English from the University of Iowa and his B.A. and M.A. in English from the University of Minnesota, where he studied with the distinguished poet-critics Allen Tate and John Berryman. He is a professor of English, emeritus, at Santa Clara University where, since 1980, he taught courses in writing and literature (including a course in writing about nature and the environment—on campus and in Trinidad & Tobago). In 1997 he received the Louis and Dorina Brutocao Award for Teaching Excellence. Professor White's other books include *Approaching Emily Dickinson, The Writer's Idea Thesaurus, The Daily Writer, The Well-Crafted Argument* (coauthored with Simone Billings), *Where Do You Get Your Ideas?* and *Writing Flash.* He lives in Folsom, California, with his wife, Therese (an attorney), and their two irrepressible cats, Emily and Otis.